D0052882

A Survey of Bible Doctrine

Charles C. Ryrie

MOODY PRESS
CHICAGO

Library of Congress Catalog Card Number: 72-77958

ISBN: 0-8024-8438-7

13 15 17 19 20 18 16 14

Printed in the United States of America

CONTENTS

This book is designed for personal study and enjoyment, but is also well-suited for use in Bible study groups.

An Important Word to Begin With

THIS IS A BOOK on Bible doctrine. We could be devious and call it by some other name like "Knowledge You Need" or "Truths for Today." But why? The word *doctrine* is a perfectly good word that simply means "teaching," and teaching is not yet in disrepute (though studying sometimes seems to be!). So let's call this book what it is — a book that will try to help you understand what the Bible teaches.

Some might think it necessary to apologize for such a book. And yet we have books like "The Teaching of Kant" (which is another way of saying "Kant's Doctrine") or "The Thought of Charles Darwin" (which is another way of labeling "Darwin's Doctrine"). Why should we apologize for investigating the teaching of a Book which was here long before Kant or Darwin, which has had a far greater circulation than any other book, and which will be around when all the others have gone out of print? Our colleges and universities rightly think it important to offer courses in psychology, sociology and education, for instance, yet all these fields of learning are relatively new in the history of man. Why, then, should anyone be embarrassed to study in the biblical field which has stood the tests which time brings to any area of learning?

Are you about to embark on a study which is or shortly will be out-of-date? The suspicion seems to be abroad that to study the Bible is a waste of time since it is a book that needs considerable updating. A person who believes that needs only to go to Israel and listen to the leaders quoting the Bible and showing how it is being fulfilled by the events occuring in that country today. Even the *Readers' Digest* in August, 1966, printed an article entitled "The Bible's Timeless Insights." It is amazing to discover how frequently and from what unexpected quarters people keep coming back to the teaching of the Bible. A study of the Bible is both contemporary and highly relevant.

The important matter suggested by the title of this chapter is simply this: Everyone has a basis of authority which becomes a base of operations for his thinking and doing. Sometimes that basis of authority is complex, for it is made up of several things; and sometimes people are ignorant of the fact that they have such a thing as a basis of authority. But everyone, without exception, has one. Let's name a few by way of illustration.

The man who believes in one of the non-Christian religions, such as Hinduism or Islam, accepts the teachings of that religion, including its writings. If he is a real disciple, he will seek to live according to its teachings. He would, of course, reject Christianity outright simply because its teachings are incompatible with what he has accepted as his basis of authority.

The principal plank in the platform of the atheist is simply that God does not exist. Acting within this frame of reference, the atheist acknowledges no revelation from any transcendent being, nor does he seek or find his code of ethics in an external authority. If he is wrong about his basic belief, then his entire system of doctrine would have to be changed. And *believe* he must, for he cannot *prove* that God does not exist.

Agnosticism seems to be little more than a popular form of atheism. Instead of the bold assertion of atheism that God does not exist, agnosticism softens the blow by affirming merely that one cannot *know* if God exists. This basic belief is the frame of reference within which the agnostic proceeds to operate. Again, his entire theology would be overthrown by the ability to know, but, like the others, he *believes* that knowing is impossible.

But we live in a day when things are not black or white, and systems of theology cannot be categorized into neat pigeonholes. For example, neoorthodoxy's basis of authority is Christ, which sounds good until you begin to investigate how substantial their idea really is. The Barthian (another name for neoorthodoxy) says that his authority is Christ and not the Bible, for that is a fallible book. But since it is a book full of errors (and if it is our only source of information about Christ), then how do we know that Christ has any authority unless we arbitrarily assign Him authority on the basis of our faith or of our reasoning? Operating within the framework of this hybrid kind of thinking, the Barthian merrily goes on his way, preaching like a conservative but believing everything that liberalism has taught through the years.

The authority of liberalism resides in man himself and especially in his reasoning processes. To the liberal, the Bible is entirely the product of human reasoning and thus contains only man's thoughts about God and the world and himself. It is the history of man's development of his religious beliefs, but it is not a message from a transcendent God who breaks into history from the outside. Ethics, then, are produced by our own minds. And while many liberals adhere to lofty codes of ethics produced by some of the best minds of history, even that one proclaimed by the noble Jesus, the basic presupposition of liberalism allows for anyone to produce his own ethical code.

Actually, that is what has happened in the "God Is Dead" theology. Even though some of these "theologians" still incorporate a "tip of the hat" to Jesus, a man or the community of men sets the guidelines for ethical conduct. They teach that if God is to reappear in the thought and life of mankind, he will do so only after we leave him dead for a while, cease talking about him, and expect that when he reappears it will be under a different label — one which men will come up with in due time. Thus, man's reason is made the seat of authority in religion. When these modern systems of theology are coupled with a belief in evolution, as they usually are, the humanistic basis of authority becomes quite concrete.

Within the Christian orbit of theological systems, Roman Catholicism, for instance, sees the Roman Church as the seat of authority. To be sure, the Bible is believed, but it must be interpreted, they say, by the church. Therefore, the church becomes the final authority, and its pronouncements are binding on its members.

The evangelical Christian's basis of authority is to be found within the framework of the revelation of God. Perhaps you are surprised that I did not say it is found in the Bible. It is, but that is only part of the revelation of God. God has revealed Himself in various ways, and all these are included in the framework which becomes the basis of authority for the Christian. God has revealed Himself in nature, in the course of history, in special events like providential actions, miracles, visions given to the prophets, etc.; but chiefly God has revealed Himself in Christ and in the Bible. Nature tells us certain things about God, but not too much really. The study of history from a Christian perspective is most rewarding, but that is not the purpose of this book. What we know of Christ we get from the Bible; therefore, a study of the Bible is the most important means by which a Christian can come to know this basis of authority which is the revelation of God.

We have noted that every other system whose basis of authority we have examined includes a large measure of faith. Therefore, it is perfectly respectable for a Christian to say, "I believe it." Now this doesn't mean that one should put his mind on the shelf while studying the teachings of his faith. Quite the contrary. The teachings of the Bible, while simple in their major outline, can be quite deep, complex, and demanding of the intellect. But always the mind will operate within a framework of the basis of authority which is the revelation of God, principally preserved in the Bible. If one thinks he is going to put his mind to rest and use it no more if he accepts the Bible, he should remember that the study of Bible doctrine could require a knowledge of Greek and Hebrew, other Semitic languages, the theological thinking of all the greats of the past, some contemporary theology, a knowledge of church history, and a few other assorted subjects. And as he progresses he will realize that God is not putting his thinking or conduct into a strait jacket, but rather, He is opening up before his thinking new areas of thought which he did not previously know existed. His perspective, too, will change, and this will give him a view of the world that will make sense.

Should someone be reading this who has some doubts about operating within this framework of authority, why not continue to read and study anyway. Would it not be fair to let the Bible speak its claims for itself before you judge concerning them? Judgment cannot be rendered with scholarly honesty unless the evidence is first heard. So even if your basis of authority has not yet jelled, why not see what the Bible has to say for itself?

In a book like this it is not possible to write out every Bible reference that supports a given doctrine. Therefore, it will be necessary for the reader to look up many of these references. Some books on Bible doctrine put a string of references after the various doctrinal points. There is nothing wrong with this, and at least it shows that there usually are plenty of Scripture passages to support the various doctrines. But the reader is often so overwhelmed with a long list of Scripture verses that he does not look up any of them. A limited number of references appear in this book, and usually they are listed in order of importance. Hopefully you will want to check on the various points to see if assertions made are really what the Bible teaches.

Before embarking on this study, here is a word of encouragement: God intended you to understand what the Bible teaches. This does not mean that you will comprehend all its truths at first reading or even in a lifetime, but it does mean that you can expect to learn a great deal. God used language which He meant to be taken just as normally and plainly as the words in this book. So take it that way and assume He means what He says. When a problem arises, look at it again and remember too that God has promised that the Holy Spirit will also help you to understand His truth (Jn 16:13; 1 Co 2:12).

1

What Is God Like?

IN THE MIDST of the knowledge explosion of the past half century, it is astounding how many have forgotten that the greatest knowledge they could possess is the knowledge of God. Suppose inhabitants of other planets were discovered; this would not be as great as knowing about the one who inhabits heaven. The fact that we have sent men to the moon is not so amazing as sending men to heaven. The knowledge of God is certainly top priority.

DOES GOD EXIST?

Traditionally there have been two lines of argument used to demonstrate the existence of God.

NATURALISTIC ARGUMENTS

The traditional line of proof is philosophical and may or may not satisfy an unbeliever. But the arguments go like this: The first is an argument from cause and effect and simply reminds people that everywhere they look in the world around them they are faced with an effect. In other words, the natural world is a result or an effect, and this forces them to account for that which caused such an effect. Actually there are two possible answers. Either (1) nothing caused this world (but the uncaused emergence of something has never been observed), or (2) something caused this world. This something may be an "eternal cosmic process," or it may be chance, or one might conclude that God was the cause. While we have to admit that this cause-

11

and-effect argument does not in itself "prove" that the God of the Bible exists, it is fair to insist that the theistic answer is less complex to believe than any other. It takes more faith to believe that evolution or blind intelligence (whatever such a contradictory phrase might mean) could have accounted for the intricate and complex world in which we live than it does to believe that God could.

The second philosophical argument concerns the purpose we see in the world. In other words, we are not only faced with a world (the first argument) but that world seems to have purpose in it. How do you account for this? The nontheist answers that this happens by chance and/or through the processes of natural selection (which are by chance too). The question remains, however: Can random "by chance" actions result in the highly integrated organization which is evident in the world about us? To say it can is possible, but it requires a great deal of faith to believe. The Christian answer may also involve faith, but it is not less believable.

The third argument concerns the nature of man. Man's conscience, moral nature, intelligence, and mental capacities have to be accounted for in some way. Again the nontheist answers that all of this evolved, and he has proposed very elaborate explanations of how this has happened. A tendency today seems to be to consider man as a biological or organic and cultural or superorganic creature and to account for the evolving of both these aspects totally by chance. But does this explain conscience or that reaching out for a belief in a higher being which seems to be universal (though terribly defective as far as understanding what that being is like)? Or does the very existence of man point to the existence of a personal God? Paul put the question this way to the philosophers of Athens: "Forasmuch then as we are the offspring of God, we ought not to think that the Godhead is like unto gold or silver, or stone, graven by art and man's device" (Ac 17:29).

In connection with this anthropological argument, the moral argument is sometimes delineated. It poses the question, How did the idea of good and bad, right and wrong ever come into human culture? Man seems to have a sense of what is desirable as opposed to what is not. Where does this sense come from, and on what basis does man decide what ought to be desired or what ought not to be? Some argue that man's recognition of good and his quest for a moral ideal point to the existence of a God who gives reality to that ideal. Others have emphasized that the ethical systems advanced by philosophers always contain contradiction and paradox if Christian theism is left out, which argues for the necessity of theism to explain satisfactorily man's idea of good and evil. For instance, the humanist declares that he does not accept any absolute standard, yet in the next breath he exhorts you to do better.

A fourth line of reasoning seems much more sophisticated and much less easy to comprehend. It is called the ontological argument (from the present participle form of the Greek verb "to be"). The idea is that God has to be since man commonly has the idea of a most perfect Being and that idea must include the existence of such a Being. The reason is simply that a being, otherwise perfect, who did not exist would not be so perfect as a being who was perfect and who did exist. Therefore, since this concept does exist in the minds of men, such a most perfect Being must exist. Or to put it another way, since God is the greatest Being who can be thought of, He cannot be conceived as not existing; for if He could, then it would be possible to conceive of a being greater than God who does exist; therefore, God must exist. Many (including Immanuel Kant) do not feel this argument has any value. It originated with Anselm in the twelfth century.

One has to face the fact that these philosophical arguments do not of themselves prove the existence of the true God. But we do not minimize them. They may be used to establish a presumption in favor of the existence of the God of the Bible, and they produce sufficient evidence to place the unregenerated man under a responsibility to accept further knowledge from God or to reject intelligently this knowledge and thus to relieve God of further obligation on his behalf. You may find that using these lines of reasoning may trigger the thinking or open the way to present the gospel more clearly to a fellow student or friend.

The entire theistic world view has come under massive attack because of the rise of mechanistic science and its questioning of the possibility of miracles and because of the popular acceptance of evolution. Evolution is discussed in chapter 7, but a word about miracles is in order here.

If a miracle is defined (as Hume did) as a violation of the laws of nature, then, of course, the possibility of a miracle happening is slim if not nil. But if a miracle is contrary to *what we know* as the laws of nature, then the possibility of introducing a new factor into the known laws of nature is not eliminated. This new miraculous factor does not contradict nature because nature is not a self-contained whole; it is only a partial system within total reality, and a miracle is consistent within that greater system which includes the supernatural. It is true, however, that a miracle is something which nature, if left to its own resources, could not produce. If one admits the postulate of God, miracles are possible. If one adds the postulates of sin and salvation and sign-evidence, then they seem necessary.

The Christian does not view miracles as an easy way out of difficulties, but as an important part of the real plot of the story of the world. Most historians will not admit the occurrence of a miracle until they have tried every other possible and less probable explanation. But the admitted improbability of a miracle happening at a given time and place does not make the story of its happening untrue or unbelievable. It is improbable that you should be the millioneth customer to enter a store and thus receive a prize, but if you are, your friends should not refuse to believe that you were simply because it was unlikely that you would be.

The dimension of the supernatural is essential to Christianity and is often seen in history. Beware when considering specific miracles that you do not slip into naturalistic explanations for them. Remember, too, that to deny miracles is to deny also the resurrection of Christ, which would mean that our faith is empty.

BIBLICAL ARGUMENTS

The other line of proof is what the Bible presents, and this may be summarized very quickly. Often it is said that the Bible does not argue for the existence of God; it simply assumes it throughout. It is true that the opening words of the Bible assume His being, and this assumption underlies and pervades every book. But it is not the whole story to say that the Bible assumes but does not argue God's existence. Look at Psalm 19 and notice that David says clearly that God has revealed His existence in the world around us. Isaiah told backslidden people who were making and worshiping idols to consider the world around them and then think whether or not idols that they made with their hands could fashion such a world. The answer is obviously negative. Then he said, "Lift up your eyes on high, and behold who hath created these things" (Is 40:26). The apostle Paul argued before a non-Christian audience that the rain and change of seasons witness to the existence of God (Ac 14:17). So the Bible does argue for as well as assume the existence of God.

How Has God Revealed Himself?

Liberalism teaches that man knows God through his own efforts. In contrast to this, one of the "good" things that Barth did when he thundered on the world his new theology was to remind men that there can be no revelation of God unless God Himself takes the initiative to make Him-

self known. In other words, the question is the one which
Zophar asked a few thousand years before, "Canst thou by
searching find out God?" (Job 11:7). The liberal says yes;
the conservative says no (this is not intended to imply that
Barth was a conservative, because he also said no; his view
of the Bible demonstrates that he was not one).

If God has taken the initiative to reveal Himself, in what
ways has He done this? We may think immediately of Christ
and the Bible as answers to this question. But there are
other answers too, like nature and history. These latter
two ways are obviously different from the former in that
they do not tell us as much about God. In other words, there
seem to be general ways and special ways in which God has
revealed Himself; the revelation of God through nature and
history is called general revelation, while other means are
labeled special revelation.

What are the characteristics of general revelation? Look
at Psalm 19:1-6. Verse 1 states the content of that revelation
as being the glory and handiwork of God. Verse 2 affirms
the continuousness of it — day and night (since the sky is
always there for man to behold). Verse 3 states the character of that revelation in nature as being a silent revelation
(the word "where" is not in the original text). Verses 4-6
tell that the coverage of that revelation is worldwide (v.
4) and to every man (note v. 6 which intimates that even
a blind man can feel the heat of the sun). Romans 1:18-
20, which is the other central passage on this doctrine, adds
the fact that the revelation of God in nature contains a
revelation of His "eternal power and Godhead." God's revelation of Himself through history comes in various ways. He
gives all people rain and productive seasons (Ac 14:17);
He especially revealed a variety of aspects of His being and
power to the nation Israel (Ps 78 — His miraculous power, v.
13; His anger, v. 21; His control of nature, v. 26; His love,
v. 38). In many ways the revelation of God through history is more explicit than that through nature.

Through Jesus Christ, God revealed Himself ("exegeted" is the word in Jn 1:18) in clarity and detail. The miracles of Christ showed things like the glory of God (Jn 2:11); His words told of the Father's care (Jn 14:2); His person showed the Father (Jn 14:9). The way to know God is to know His Son; and apart from the revelation through the Son, little is known of God.

The other avenue of special revelation is the Bible. Today some are saying that the Bible is a lesser revelation than the Son, and to make too much of it is to worship the Bible (bibliolatry). But if we do not make much of the Bible, then we cannot know much of the Son, for our only source of information about the Son (and hence about the Father) is through the Bible. Furthermore, if the Bible is not to be trusted, then again we cannot know truth about the Son. Or if only certain parts of the Bible are trustworthy, we will end up with as many pictures of Christ as there are people picking the parts of the biography which they think are reliable. In other words, if the Bible is not completely true, we end up with either misinformation or subjective evaluation. Jesus Himself asserted that the Bible revealed Him (Lk 24:27, 44-45; Jn 5:39). And, of course, the Bible reveals many other things about God. Think, for instance, of the many aspects of His plan which are known only through the Bible and which tell us about Him. You might say that the Bible is an inexhaustible source of information about God.

WHAT IS GOD LIKE?

With all these channels of revelation we ought to be able to learn something about what God is like. Traditionally, the characteristics of God stated formally and systematically are called the attributes of God; and traditionally, they have been divided into two categories. There are some ways in which God is like us (for instance, God is just, and man can be just too); and there are some ways in which God is unique (for instance, He is infinite, which finds no correspondence in us). However, these categories are not hard and fast, and some of the choices as to which attributes to place within which category are debatable. The important thing to study is the attribute itself to learn not only what it reveals about God but also what implications that it has for one's personal outlook and life.

1. *God is omniscient.* Omniscience means that God knows everything, and this includes the knowledge not only of things that actually happen but also of things which might happen. This kind of knowledge God had by nature and without the effort of learning. Jesus claimed omniscience when He said, "If the mighty works, which were done in you, had been done in Tyre and Sidon, they would have repented long ago in sackcloth and ashes" (Mt 11: 21). Here is a display of the knowledge of things that might have happened. God "telleth the number of the stars; he calleth them all by their names" (Ps 147:4), and "known unto God are all his works from the beginning of the world" (Ac 15:18).

The practical ramifications of the omniscience of God are many. Think, for instance, what this means in relation to the eternal security of the believer. If God knows all, then obviously nothing can come to light subsequent to our salvation which He did not know when He saved us. There were no skeletons in the closet which He did not know about when He offered to give us eternal salvation. Think again what omniscience means when something tragic occurs in our lives. God knows and has known all about it from the beginning and is working all things out for His glory and our ultimate good. Consider what omniscience ought to mean in relation to living the Christian life. Here is Someone who knows all the pitfalls as well as the ways to be happy and who has offered to give us this wisdom. If we would heed what He says then we could avoid a lot of trouble and experience a lot of happiness.

2. *God is holy.* The word *holiness* is very difficult to define. The dictionary does not help much since it just defines holiness as absence of evil, and it is usually measured against a relative standard. In God, holiness is certainly absence of evil, but it must also include a positive righteousness and all of this measured against Himself as an absolute standard. Holiness is one of the most important, if not the most important, attributes of God, and certainly nothing that God does can be done apart from being in complete harmony with His holy nature. Peter declares that "he which hath called you is holy" (1 Pe 1:15), and then he goes on to state what effect that should have in our lives, namely, "so be ye holy in all manner of conversation [life]."

An analogy may help in understanding this concept of holiness. What does it mean to be healthy? It means more than not being sick. Likewise, holiness is more than absence of sin; it is a positive, healthy state of being right. This is what John meant when he said that God is light (1 Jn 1:5).

The ramification of this is obvious: "Walk in the light." A proper concept of holiness as a requirement for Christian living would end a lot of discussion about what is permitted to the Christian and what is not. It seems as though many are trying to discover how close they can come to sin without being cut off from their particular Christian group or clique instead of determining the propriety of things on the simple basis of "Is it holy?" Don't be tempted to be a leader in or follower of the "let's skate on as thin ice as possible" group; instead, be a leader in holiness. This will please God because it imitates Him.

3. *God is just (or righteousness).* While holiness principally concerns the character of God, justice or righteousness has more to do with the character expressed in His dealings with men. It means that God is equitable, or, as the Bible puts it, He is no respecter of persons. David said,

"The judgments of the LORD are true and righteous alto-gether" (Ps 19:9; see also Ps 116:5; 145:17; Jer 12:1).

The most obvious application of the justice of God is in connection with judgment. When men stand before God to be judged they will receive full justice. This is both a comfort (for those who have been wronged in life) and a warning (for those who think they have been getting away with evil). Before an unsaved audience Paul emphatically warned of the coming righteous judgment: "He hath appointed a day, in the which he will judge the world in righteousness by that man whom he hath ordained; whereof he hath given assurance unto all men, in that he hath raised him from the dead" (Ac 17:31).

If you think a little further you might ask if God can save sinners and still be just. This is a good question and is answered by Paul in Romans 3:21-26 in the affirmative, but only because (as he explains) Jesus died to pay the penalty for sin which a just God required. But the price having been paid, God can be just (not compromising His holiness) and at the same time justify the one who believes in Jesus.

4. *God is love* (*1 Jn 4:8*). What is love? This is one of the most often used and most infrequently defined words in our vocabulary today. Here is one way of arriving at a proper concept of what love is. When young people think of love they think first and quite naturally of a pleasant emotional experience. And this *is* love, but it is not the whole concept. When those same young people grow up, marry, and have children, they soon learn that they have to discipline those children. The couple that first cuddles a baby and then soon after corrects that baby who, for instance, reaches out to touch a hot stove, is expressing two aspects of love. So any definition of love must be broad enough to include both the cuddling and correcting aspects of love. Therefore, we might tentatively propose the definition that love is that which seeks good for the object loved. But anyone who rears children knows that there are as

many experts on child-rearing as there are grandmothers and aunts. What is good in the opinion of one is not good in the judgment of another. For the Christian this problem of what is good is easily solved. *Good* is the will of God. So, putting that in our tentative definition, we may say that love is that which seeks the will of God in the object loved. Will such a definition work? Let's test it. God is love, meaning that He seeks His own will or glory, and we know that this is true. God loves the world, meaning that He seeks to have His will followed by the world. God loves sinners, meaning He wants them to know His will, and it is His desire that they believe on His Son. We are to love one another, meaning that we are to endeavor to see that the will of God is done in each other. So the definition seems to work.

The love of God seems to be of such a nature as to interest itself in the welfare of creatures in a measure beyond any normal human conception (1 Jn 3:16; Jn 3:16). It is almost beyond human comprehension to think of God allowing Himself to become emotionally involved with human beings. Of course the great manifestation of this was in the sacrifice of His Son for the salvation of men (1 Jn 4:9-10). The Bible also teaches that the love of God is shed abroad in the hearts of the children of God (Ro 5:8).

There is a very popular teaching today that says that because God is love and always acts in a loving manner toward His creatures, eventually all men will be saved. This teaching is called universalism. The trouble with the doctrine is not only that it contradicts direct statements of the Bible which say that men will be cast into hell forever (Mk 9:45-48), but it misunderstands the concept of love and its relation to the other attributes of God. Love may have to punish, and the attribute of love does not operate in God apart from His other attributes, particularly the attributes of holiness and justice.

5. *God is true.* Truth is another concept which is difficult to define. The dictionary says that it is agreement

which is represented; if applied to God, it means that God is consistent with Himself and thus everything He does is true also. The Bible asserts that God is true (Ro 3:4) and Jesus claimed to be the truth (Jn 14:6), thus making Himself equal with God. The ramifications of the truthfulness of God lie chiefly in the area of His promises. He cannot be false to any one of the promises He has made. This includes broad and inclusive promises as, for instance, to the nation Israel, and it affects with equal certainty the promises made to believers for daily living. The truth of God also affects His revelation, for He who is true cannot and has not revealed anything false to us.

6. *God is free.* Freedom in God means that He is independent of all His creatures, but it obviously could not mean that He is independent of Himself. Often we hear it said that the only restrictions on God are those inherent in His own person (e.g., God cannot sin because His holiness restricts Him from doing that). Perhaps it would be better to consider the matter in this fashion: the only restrictions on God's freedom are the restrictions of perfection, and since perfection is no restriction, in reality, then, God is not restricted in any way. When Isaiah asked the people, Who has directed the Lord or who has taught Him anything or who has instructed Him? (Is 40:13-14), He expected the answer "no one," because God is free (independent of His creatures). If this be true, then anything God has done for His creatures is not out of a sense of obligation to them, for He has none. What He has done for us is out of His love and compassion for us.

7. *God is omnipotent.* Fifty-six times the Bible declares that God is the almighty one (and this word is used of no one but God, cf. Rev 19:6). When students talk about the omnipotence of God they often joke about it along the line of asking if God could make two plus two equal six. The trouble with such a question is simply that it is not in the realm which omnipotence is concerned with. You might

as well ask if dynamite could make two plus two equal six. The truths of mathematics are not in the area of omnipotence. But the security of the believer certainly is, and we are kept secure in our salvation by an omnipotent God (1 Pe 1:5). In fact, our salvation comes because the gospel is the power of God unto salvation (Ro 1:16). So rather than meditating on the ridiculous, let's be thankful for the basics of our redemption which are effected by the power of God. Furthermore, God's omnipotence is seen in His power to create (Gen 1:1), in His preservation of all things (Heb 1: 3), and in His providential care for us.

8. *God is infinite and eternal.* Since there is nothing in our human natures which corresponds to *infinity* (only the opposite, finitude), it is difficult, if not impossible, for us to comprehend the term. Indeed, most dictionaries resort to defining it by negatives — without termination or without finitude. *Eternity* is usually defined as infinity related to time. Whatever is involved in these concepts, we can see that they must mean God is not bound by the limitations of finitude and He is not bound by the succession of events, which is a necessary part of time. Also His eternality extends backward from our viewpoint of time as well as forward forever. Nevertheless, this concept does not mean that time is unreal to God. Although He sees the past and future as clearly as the present, He sees them as including succession of events, without being Himself bound by that succession. "Before the mountains were brought forth, or ever thou hadst formed the earth and the world, even from everlasting to everlasting, thou art God" (Ps 90:2; cf. Gen 21:33; Ac 17:24).

9. *God is immutable.* Immutability means that God is unchanging and unchangeable. God never differs from Himself, and thus in our concept of God there can be no idea of a growing or developing being. He is the one in whom is no variableness (Ja 1:17; cf. Mal 3:6; Is 46:9-10). There is a problem in connection with the immutability

of God, and it concerns verses which say that God repented (Gen 6:6; Jon 3:10). If these verses are understood to mean that there actually was a change in God's plans, then He is either not immutable or not sovereign. But if such verses refer only to the revelation or unfolding of God's plans to men, then it can be said that although His plan does not change, as man views its unfolding it seems to involve change. In other words, God's "repentance" is only from our viewpoint; therefore, it is only apparent repentance as His eternal and unchanging plan is worked out in history.

10. *God is omnipresent.* Omnipresence means simply that God is everywhere present. That concept is not difficult, but some aspects related to it are. For instance, what is the difference between omnipresence and pantheism? Essentially, it is this: Omnipresence says God is everywhere present (though separate from the world and the things in it), while pantheism says that God is *in* everything. Omnipresence says that God is present in the room where you are reading this, while pantheism affirms that God is in the chair and in the window, etc. Another important distinction is this: Even though God *is* everywhere (though not *in* everything), this does not contradict the fact that there are varying degrees of the manifestation of His presence. God's presence in the Shekinah glory was an immediate and localized manifestation of His presence, while His presence in relation to unredeemed men is scarcely realized by them. Furthermore, the presence of God is not usually in visible or bodily form. Occasionally He has appeared so that His glory was seen, but omnipresence is a spiritual manifestation of God. Psalm 139 teaches His omnipresence in a most vivid way, and of course this doctrine means that no one can escape God. If people try throughout their entire lifetime, they still cannot escape Him at death. On the other hand, it also means that a believer may experience the presence of God at all times and know the blessing of walking with Him in every trial and circumstance of life.

11. *God is sovereign.* The word *sovereign* means chief, highest or supreme. When we say that God is sovereign we are saying that He is the number one Ruler in the universe. Actually, the word itself does not tell anything about how that Ruler may rule, although this is described in the Bible. The word itself means only that He is the supreme Being in the universe. Of course, the position brings with it a certain amount of authority, and in God's case that authority is total and absolute. This does not mean, however, that He rules His universe as a dictator, for God is not only sovereign, He is also love and holiness. He can do nothing apart from the exercise of all His attributes acting harmoniously together. The concept of sovereignty involves the entire plan of God in all of its intricate details of design and outworking. Although He often allows things to take their natural course according to laws which He designed, it is the sovereign God who is working all things according to His wise plan.

That the Bible teaches the sovereignty of God there can be no doubt. Just read Ephesians 1 and Romans 9 (and don't worry about all the ramifications). For the Christian the idea of sovereignty is an encouraging one, for it assures him that nothing is out of God's control, and that His plans do triumph.

These are the principal attributes or characteristics of God, and this is the only God that exists. The God of the Bible is not a god of man's own making or thinking or choosing, but He is the God of His own revelation.

WHAT DOES GOD CALL HIMSELF?

A person's names always tell something about him or about the relationship he has to those who use the names. Often names grow out of experiences people have. So it is with God. He has revealed aspects of His nature by the names He uses with men, and some of them have grown out of specific experiences men have had with God.

PRIMARY OLD TESTAMENT NAMES

1. *Elohim.* The most general (and least specific in significance) name for God in the Old Testament is Elohim. Although its etymology is not clear, it apparently means "Strong One," and it is used not only of the true God but also of heathen gods (Gen 31:30; Ex 12:12). The *im* ending indicates that the word is plural, and this has given rise to considerable speculation as to the significance of the plural. Some have suggested that it is an indication of polytheism, which would be difficult to sustain since the singular (*Eloah*) is rarely used and since Deuteronomy 6:4 clearly says that God is one. Others have attempted to prove the concept of the Trinity from this plural word. While the doctrine of the Trinity is of course a biblical one, it is very doubtful that it can be proved on the basis of this name for God. Nevertheless, this is not to say that the plural Elohim in no way indicates some distinctions within the Godhead. Though the plural does allow for the subsequent clear revelation of the Trinity in the New Testament, it most likely is best understood as indicating fullness of power. Elohim, the strong one, is the powerful Governor of the universe and of all the affairs of mankind. This name for God occurs over 2,500 times in the Old Testament. Take time to read verses like Genesis 1:1 and remember that this one is your God in all the circumstances of life.

2. *Jehovah.* This is the most specific name for God in the Old Testament, though Jehovah is not a real word! It is actually an artificial English word put together from the four Hebrew consonants YHWH and the vowels from another name for God, *Adonai.* Thus Jehovah was concocted this way: YaHoWaH, or Jehovah. The Jews had a superstitious dread of pronouncing the name YHWH, so whenever they came to it they said Adonai. We probably ought to pronounce it Yahweh.

The meaning of the word is also a matter of much discussion. There seems to be agreement that it is connected somehow with the Hebrew verb, *to be,* or some variant or earlier form of it, so that it does have the idea of God's eternal self-existence (Ex 3:14). In its use in Exodus 6:6, however, there seems to be an added idea that connects this name in a special way with God's power to redeem Israel out of Egyptian bondage. We have already seen that a name usually tells something about a person and some relationship that person has. In the name *Yahweh* these two features of a name are evident: Yahweh is eternal, and Yahweh bore a special relationship to Israel as her Redeemer.

The name occurs nearly 7,000 times in the Old Testament and is especially associated with Yahweh's holiness (Lev 11:44-45), with His hatred of sin (Gen 6:3-7) and with His gracious provision of redemption (Is 53:1, 5, 6, 10).

3. *Adonai.* This is the name of God which the Jews substituted for the Tetragrammaton (the four letters YHWH, Yahweh) when they read the Scriptures. Yet it, too, is a basic designation for God and means Lord (master). It is used, as one might expect, of the relationship between men (like master and slave, as in Ex 21:1-6); thus when it refers to God's relationship with men it conveys the idea of His absolute authority. Notice its occurrences in Joshua 5:14 (where Joshua recognized the authority of the captain of the Lord's hosts) and Isaiah 6:8-11 (where Isaiah was commissioned by his Master).

There are two sides to a master-servant relationship. On the one hand, the servant must give absolute obedience to his master. On the other hand the master obligates himself to take care of the servant. If the believer truthfully calls God by His name, Lord, then he can expect God to take care of him, and God in turn can expect the believer to obey Him in everything.

COMPOUND OLD TESTAMENT NAMES

Frequently the Old Testament reveals something about the character or activity of God by using some designation in compound with Yahweh or El (which is the singular of Elohim). Here are some examples:

1. *El Elyon* — *"The most high"* (Gen 14:22). Notice its use in connection with Lucifer's desire to be like the Most High (Is 14:14).

2. *El Olam* — *"The everlasting God"* (Gen 21:33). Notice this use in connection with God's inexhaustible strength (Is 40:28).

3. *El Shaddai* — *"The Almighty God"* (Gen 17:1). This probably derives from a related word which means "mountain" and pictures God as the overpowering almighty one standing on a mountain. The name is often used in connection with the chastening of God's people, as in Ruth 1:20-21 and the thirty-one times it is used in the book of Job.

4. *Yahweh Jireh* — *The Lord provides* (Gen 22:14). This is the only occurrence. After the angel of the Lord pointed to a ram as a substitute for Isaac, Abraham named the place, "the Lord provides."

5. *Yahweh Nissi* — *The Lord is my Banner* (Ex 17:15). Similarly, after the defeat of the Amalekites, Moses erected an altar and called it Yahweh Nissi. Actually this and the other compounds are not really names of God, but designations that grew out of commemorative events.

6. *Yahweh Shalom* — *The Lord is peace* (Judg 6:24).

7. *Yahweh Sabbaoth* — *"The LORD of hosts"* (1 Sa 1:3). The hosts are the angels of heaven which are ready to obey the Lord's commands. This title was often used by the prophets (Isaiah and Jeremiah) during times of national distress to remind the people that Yahweh was still their Protector.

8. *Yahweh Maccaddeshcem* — *The Lord thy Sanctifier* (Ex 31:13).

9. *Yahweh Roi* — *"The LORD . . . my shepherd"* (Ps 23:1).

10. *Yahweh Tsidkenu* — *The Lord our Righteousness* (Jer 23:6). This title was a direct thrust against King

Zedekiah (which means Yahweh is righteousness) who was a completely unrighteous king (2 Ch 36:12-13).

11. *Yahweh Shammah* — "*The* LORD *is there*" (Eze 48: 35).

12. *Yahweh Elohim Israel* — "*The* LORD *God of Israel*" (Judg 5:3). This is a designation frequently used by the prophets (Is 17:6), similar to the God of Abraham, Isaac and Jacob.

13. *Qadosh Israel* — "*The Holy One of Israel*" (Is 1:4).

This list might go on and on because these compounds are not really distinct names but are more designations or titles. Yet they need to be included in our study since they do reveal some things about God. Remember, in the East a name is more than an identification; it is descriptive of its bearer, often revealing some characteristic or activity of that person. "O LORD, our Lord, how excellent is thy name in all the earth!" (Ps 8:1, 9).

To review: The knowledge of the true God is the highest knowledge any person can have. There are certain logical arguments which can at least tip the balance in favor of theism (though they do not tell us who God is or what He is like). The world around us tells us of the power of God, but it is from the Bible that we learn the full facts about God. Specifically we learn about Him through what the Bible says about His character (attributes) and His names.

WHAT IS THE TRINITY?

The word *trinity* is not found in the Bible; indeed, many think it is a poor word to use to try to describe this particular teaching of the Bible. Actually, it describes only half the teaching; the reason will become clear shortly.

When you study a book like this, it may appear to you that the writer, or the church, or somebody else is saying to you, "Here are the doctrines — believe them!" If that's the case it is only because you are looking at the results of someone's study, not the process of it. We are not saying,

"Here are some doctrines to be believed whether you like it or not," but rather, "Here are some facts to be faced. How would you harmonize and organize them?"

The teaching on the Trinity is a good illustration of this point. You have probably heard lessons on the Trinity in which you were taught only the results: that the one God exists in three Persons. Then you asked for illustrations and got none that were satisfying. So you concluded that there was a doctrine you were expected to believe — regardless! Actually, the way we ought to go about it is this: as we read the Bible, certain astounding facts confront us and demand our attention. Specifically, the Bible seems to say clearly that there is only one true God. But it also seems to say with equal clarity that there was a man Jesus Christ who claimed equality with God and there is Someone called the Holy Spirit who is also equal with God. Now how do you put those facts together? The way conservatives have put them together results in the doctrine of the Trinity. Others have put these facts together and have come up with a different idea of the Trinity (the Persons being modes of expression of God and not distinct persons), and still others, rejecting the claims of Christ and the Spirit to be God, become unitarians. But the claims are still there in the Bible, and the need for packaging them is what we study in this section.

Any concept of the Trinity must be carefully balanced, for it must maintain on the one side the unity of God, and on the other, the distinctness and equality of the Persons. That is why the word *trinity* only tells half of the doctrine — the "threeness" part and not the unity. Perhaps the word *tri-unity* is better since it contains both ideas — the "tri" (the threeness) and the "unity" (the oneness).

EVIDENCE FOR ONENESS

Deuteronomy 6:4 may be translated various ways (e.g., "Yahweh our God is one Yahweh," or "Yahweh is our God,

Yahweh alone"), but in any case it is a strong declaration of monotheism. So are Deuteronomy 4:35 and 32:39 as well as Isaiah 45:14 and 46:9. The first of the so-called Ten Commandments shows that Israel was expected to understand that there is only one true God (Ex 20:3; Deu 5:7). The New Testament is equally clear in passages like 1 Corinthians 8:4-6, Ephesians 4:3-6 and James 2:19, all of which state emphatically that there is only one true God. Therefore, the doctrine of the Trinity must not imply in any way that there might be three Gods. God is single and unique, demanding the exclusion of all pretended rivals and removing any hint of tritheism.

EVIDENCE FOR THREENESS

Nowhere does the New Testament explicitly state the doctrine of triunity (since 1 Jn 5:7 is apparently not a part of the genuine text of Scripture), yet the evidence is overwhelming.

1. The Father is recognized as God. Notice, among many Scripture verses, John 6:27 and 1 Peter 1:2. This point is seldom debated.

2. Jesus Christ is recognized as God. Doubting Thomas recognized Him as such (Jn 20:28). He Himself claimed some of the attributes which only God has, like omniscience (Mt 9:4), omnipotence (Mt 28:18) and omnipresence (Mt 28:20). Further, He did things which only God can do (and the people recognized this) (Mk 2:1-12 — healing the paralytic was done to prove that Christ had the power to forgive sins which was acknowledged as something only God can do).

3. The Holy Spirit is recognized as God. He is spoken of as God (Ac 5:3-4 — lying to the Spirit is the same as lying to God). He possesses the same attributes as God and those which belong exclusively to God (omniscience, 1 Co 2:10; omnipresence, Ps 139:7). It is the Spirit who regenerates man (Jn 3:5-6, 8).

This New Testament evidence is quite clear and explicit. Is there any similar evidence in the Old Testament? The answer is no, because what the Old Testament reveals concerning the Trinity is not clear and explicit but intimating and implicit. It is probably best to say that the Old Testament, although it does not reveal the triunity of God, does allow for the later New Testament revelation of it. Passages which use the plural word for God, Elohim, and plural pronouns of God allow for this subsequent revelation (Gen 1:1, 26). The Angel of Yahweh is recognized as God and yet is distinct from God (Gen 22:15-16), indicating two equal Persons. The Messiah is called the mighty God (Is 9:6 and note eternality ascribed to Him in Mic 5:2) again indicating two equal yet distinct Persons. Probably Isaiah 48:16 is the clearest intimation of the Trinity in the Old Testament because "I" — the Lord — is associated with God and the Spirit in an apparently equal relationship. But still these are only intimations and are not so explicit as the New Testament evidences.

THE EVIDENCE FOR TRIUNITY

Probably the verse that best states the doctrine of the triunity of God balancing both aspects of the concept, the unity and the Trinity, is Matthew 28:19, "baptizing them in the name of the Father, and of the Son, and of the Holy Ghost." There is no question about the "threeness" aspect, for the Father, Son and Spirit are mentioned — and only three. The unity is strongly indicated in the singular "name" rather than "names." There are other verses similar to this one where the three are associated in equality and yet distinguished (like the benediction in 2 Co 13:14 and the presence of the Trinity at the baptism of Christ, Mt 3:16-17), but they do not also contain the strong emphasis on unity as indicated in the singular "name" in Matthew 28:19.

Having looked at the evidence and having concluded that

there is one God and yet three Persons in the Godhead, is it possible to formalize this concept in a definition? Warfield's is one of the best: "The doctrine that there is one only and true God, but in the unity of the Godhead there are three eternal and co-equal Persons, the same in substance but distinct in subsistence." Subsistence means being or existence. The word *person* is really not so good, because it seems to indicate separate individuals in the Godhead; but, though we all recognize deficiency in the word, what better one is there?

Can the Trinity be illustrated? Not perfectly, nor probably very well, because most illustrations cannot include the idea that the three fully possess all the qualities of the one equally and without separation. One illustration from psychology notes that the innermost being of man — his soul — can carry on dialogue with itself, noting both sides of the debate and making judgments. Another uses the sun (like the Father) and notes that we only see the light of the sun, not the sun itself, which yet possesses all the properties of the sun (like the Son who came to earth), and observing further that the chemical power of the sun (which also possesses all the qualities of the sun and yet is distinct) is what makes plants grow. The sun, its light, and its power may give some help in illustrating the Trinity.

It is no wonder that a difficult doctrine like this has been the focal point of many errors throughout church history. One error that crops up again and again sees the Spirit as a mere influence and not a living person who is God. Sometimes Christ, too, is regarded as inferior to the Father, even as is some created being (dynamic Monarchianism, Arianism, present-day Unitarianism). Another error regards the concept of the Trinity as merely modes or manifestations of God (Sabellianism, after Sabellius, *c.* A.D. 250, or modalism). Karl Barth was for all intents and purposes a modalist, though he often rejected the label.

Is the teaching important? How else could you conceive

of our atonement being accomplished apart from a triune God? God becoming man, living, dying, raised from the dead is pretty hard to conceive of if you are a Unitarian. Does not this doctrine illuminate the concept of fellowship? The fact that God is Father, Son and Spirit emphasizes the fact that He is a God of love and fellowship within His own being. And this is the one with whom we as believers can enjoy fellowship as well.

THE FATHER

Since the Son and the Holy Spirit are considered in detail later, we need to add a word here concerning the particular relationships and works of the Father.

THE PARTICULAR RELATIONSHIPS OF THE FATHER

1. All people are called the offspring of God (Ac 17:29); therefore, there is a sense in which God is the Father of all men as their Creator. This is simply a creature-Creator relationship and is in no sense a spiritual one.

2. God is the Father of the nation Israel (Ex 4:22). Not all in Israel were redeemed, so this relationship was both spiritual (with believers) and governmental (with all in Israel, whether believers or not).

3. God is the Father of the Lord Jesus Christ (Mt 3:17).

4. In a very special way God is the Father of all who believe in Christ (Gal 3:26).

THE PARTICULAR WORKS OF THE FATHER

Almost everything God does involves in some way or other all the Members of the Trinity. So when we speak of the particular works of the Father we are not excluding the other Persons, but simply delineating those things which seem to be the prerogative of the Father in a special way.

1. It is the Father who was the Author of the decree or plan of God (Ps 2:7-9).

2. The Father was related to the act of election as its Author (Eph 1:3-6).

3. The Father sent the Son to this world (Jn 5:37).

4. The Father is the disciplinarian of His children (Heb 12:9).

IMPORTANT RAMIFICATIONS OF THE DOCTRINE OF GOD

Two final thoughts:

1. There is no other God but the one we have been trying to describe. Gods of our making, whether radically different from the God of the Bible or akin to Him, are false. Even good Christians can fall into the trap of trying to mold God according to their own thinking or wishes or pleasure. The result may be a god not dissimilar to the God of the Bible, but it will not be the true God. We know God not because we can initiate or generate such knowledge, but because He has revealed Himself. Therefore, what we know does not come from our minds but from His revelation. Beware of creating a god!

2. If the true God is as He is revealed to be, then it shouldn't be hard for us to believe that He could perform miracles, give us an inspired Bible, become incarnate, or take over the kingdoms of this world. In other words, if we accept the facts about the true God which have been revealed, then it shouldn't be difficult to believe He could and can do what is claimed of Him. That is why the knowledge of God takes first priority in the study of doctrine.

2

Is the Bible Inspired?

IN THE INTRODUCTION to this book, we pointed out that every man has a basis of authority on which he thinks and acts. For the Christian this is the Bible, which is claimed to be a book that is different from all others. Let's examine this claim.

The English word *Bible* is derived from the Greek word which means "roll" or "book" — actually a roll of papyrus (Lk 4:17; Dan 9:2). The term *scripture* is used in the New Testament of the sacred books of the Old Testament which were regarded as inspired (2 Ti 3:16; and Ro 3:2) and also of other parts of the New Testament (2 Pe 3:16). The phrase, "Word of God," is used in the New Testament of both Old and New Testaments in written form (Mt 15:6, ASV; Jn 10:35; Heb 4:12). Each of these terms refers to the Book *par excellence,* the unique and recognized record of God's revelation to man.

By some very obvious tests the Bible is a unique book. It was written over a period of 1,500 years by about 40 different authors, and yet it is one book without contradictions in what it says. And what it says is remarkable, for it speaks with equal ease and authority of the known and unknowable, of the pleasant and unpleasant, of man's accomplishments and failures, of the past and the future. Few books ever attempt such scope; none is completely accurate except the Bible.

THE MEANING AND MEANS OF REVELATION

The word *revelation* simply means "unveiling." It is often defined in relation to the Bible as God making known to men what otherwise would be unknown. However, this is really

not a good definition because there are many things in the
Bible which were known simply because men were eye-
witnesses to the events. But there are also many things
that we would never know except for divine revelation. The
word is also used in 1 Corinthians 2:10 in the sense of the
illuminating work of the Spirit. Thus revelation can be
through natural means or supernatural means; it can relate
to persons or propositions; it can refer to particular parts
of the Bible ("God revealed the future to the prophets") or
to the entire Bible, and it can refer to the content of the Bible or to the interpretation of that content (illumination).

The means of revelation have generally been divided into
the two categories: general and special revelation. General
revelation includes all means apart from Christ and the Bible; that is, God's revelation through nature (Ro 1:18-21),
through His providential dealings with man (Ro 8:28), and
through His preservation of the universe (Col 1:17), and
man's moral nature (Gen 1:26; Ac 17:29). Special revelation is that which has come through Christ (Jn 1:18) and
through the Bible (1 Jn 5:9-12). General revelation is
sufficient to alert a man to his need of God and to condemn
him if he rejects what he can learn through nature, but
only faith in Christ is sufficient to save (Ac 4:12). If this
does not seem fair, look at it this way: Suppose you knew
of a student who needed $400 to pay his school bill, and
you gave him $3 to help pay that debt (the $3 being more
than you could really afford). If he returned it to you,
asking sarcastically what good that little bit would do toward a $400 debt, would you feel any obligation at all to
give him $100 the next day if you received a large gift in the
mail? Undoubtedly not. But if he gratefully took the $3 you
offered, you would be anxious to help him further as soon as
you were able. Just so, God's general revelation if rejected
brings just condemnation; but if accepted, then He will
bring the further necessary message of the gospel in order
that that man might be saved (Ac 10:3-6).

WHAT IS MEANT BY "INSPIRATION"?

Revelation concerns the material or content by which God is disclosed, and inspiration concerns the record of that content, the Bible. Strictly speaking, *inspiration* means to fill or breathe into. In 2 Timothy 3:16 the word translated "inspiration" is more accurately "spiration," that is, "God-breathed." In other words, the verse simply says that Scripture is God-produced and it does not actually indicate any of the means that God may have used in producing it.

A DEFINITION

My own definition of biblical inspiration is that it is God's superintendence of the human authors so that, using their own individual personalities, they composed and recorded without error His revelation to man in the words of the original autographs. Several features of the definition are worth emphasizing: (1) God superintended but did not dictate the material. (2) He used human authors and their own individual styles. (3) Nevertheless, the product was, in its original manuscripts, without error.

VIEWS OF INSPIRATION

Not all agree with the above definition and its implications.

1. Some hold that the writers of the Bible were men of great genius, but that their writings were inspired no more than those of other geniuses throughout history. This has been called the view of *natural inspiration,* for there is no supernatural dimension to it.

2. A step up is the view which may be labeled the *mystical or illumination* view of inspiration, which sees the writers of the Bible as Spirit-filled and guided believers just as any believer may be even today. Logically, one might conclude that any Spirit-filled Christian could write Scripture today. Similar to this is the idea that the biblical writers were inspired to a greater *degree* than others.

3. The usual charicature of verbal inspiration is that it means *dictation;* that is, the writers were completely passive and God simply dictated to them what was to be recorded. Of course it is true that some parts of the Bible were dictated (like the Ten Commandments and the rest of the law), but the definition proposed above incorporates the idea that God allowed the writers varying degrees of self-expression as they wrote.

4. *Partial inspiration* views certain parts of the Bible as supernaturally inspired, namely, portions which would otherwise have been unknowable (accounts of creation, prophecy, etc.).

5. A very popular concept of inspiration is that only the *concepts* but not the very words were inspired. This seems to allow for a measure of authority without the necessity of the words being completely accurate.

6. The *neoorthodox* or Barthian view of inspiration is that the Bible is a witness to the Word of God, though a Barthian would not be adverse to saying also that the Bible is the Word of God. But this is true only in a secondary sense (Christ being primarily the Word), and his Bible is full of errors because it is merely the product of fallible writers. The Barthian accepts the teachings of liberalism concerning the Bible and then tries to give it a measure of authority on the ground that in a fallible way it does point to Christ.

7. Among many conservatives today a view is held that might be labeled the *inspired purpose* view of the Bible. This simply means that while the Bible contains factual errors and insoluble discrepancies in its content, it does have "doctrinal integrity" and thus accomplishes perfectly God's purpose for it. Those who hold this idea can and do use the words *infallible* and *inerrant,* but it is important to notice that they carefully limit the Bible's infallibility to the main purpose or principal emphasis of the Bible and do not extend it to include the accuracy of all its historical facts and parallel accounts. One recent writer put it this way: "I

confess the infallibility and inerrancy of the Scriptures in accomplishing God's purpose for them — to give man the revelation of God in His redemptive love through Jesus Christ."[1] In other words, the principal revelation of God — salvation — has been transmitted infallibly by means of the records which, nevertheless, are quite fallible. In contrast to Barthians, those who hold this concept of inspiration would hold a more conservative view toward matters like authorship and dates of the books of the Bible and would in general consider the Bible as a whole more trustworthy. But it is still fallible and errant; and if that be so in historical matters, who can be sure it is not also fallible in doctrinal matters? Besides, how can one separate doctrine and history? Try to in relation to the great events of Christ's life. Those doctrines depend on the accuracy of the historical facts.

THE BIBLICAL TESTIMONY

Just to illustrate how times have changed, not many years ago all one had to say to affirm his belief in the full inspiration of the Bible was that he believed it was "the Word of God." Then it became necessary to add "the inspired Word of God." Later he had to include "the verbally, inspired Word of God." Then to mean the same thing he had to say "the plenary (fully), verbally, inspired Word of God." Then came the necessity to say "the plenary, verbally, infallible, inspired Word of God." Today one has to say "the plenary, verbally, infallible, inspired, and inerrant-in-the original-manuscripts Word of God." And even then, he may not communicate clearly!

What does the Bible claim for itself?

1. It claims that all Scripture is God-breathed (2 Ti 3: 16). This means that God, who is true (Ro 3:4), breathed out truth.

2. But did man corrupt that truth in the process of recording it? No, for the Bible also testifies that the men who

wrote were "carried along by the Holy Spirit" (2 Pe 1:21, TEV). The Spirit, thus, became a Coauthor with each human writer of the Bible. Notice a number of places in the New Testament where portions of the Old Testament which were written by various men are assigned to the Holy Spirit as the Author. The only way to account for this phenomenon is to recognize a dual authorship (see Mk 12: 36, where the Spirit is said to be the Author of what David wrote in Ps 110; Ac 1:16 and 4:24-25, where Ps 41 and Ps 2 are ascribed to the Holy Spirit; and Heb 3:7; 10:15-16).

3. But sometimes the record quite obviously reflects the styles and expressions of the human authors. This is to be expected in a book of dual authorship, and does not mean at all that in employing their own styles the authors recorded error (see Ro 9:1-3 for one such example).

4. Indeed, the Bible seems to claim inerrancy for itself. How else is it possible to explain the Lord's claim for the abiding character of the letters which spell the words of Scripture: "For verily I say unto you, Till heaven and earth pass, one jot or one tittle shall in no wise pass from the law, till all be fulfilled" (Mt 5:18)? The jot is the Hebrew letter *yod,* the smallest one in that alphabet. The tittle is the minor stroke that distinguishes certain Hebrew letters from others (like a *dalet* from a *res*). In a normal font of type it would not be more than 1/16 of an inch. In other words, the Lord was saying that every letter or every word is important, and the Old Testament would be fulfilled exactly as spelled out letter by letter and word by word.

The Lord also insisted on the importance of a present tense in Matthew 22:32. In order to reinforce the truth of resurrection, He reminded the Sadducees that God *is* the God of the living because He identified Himself to Moses by saying "I *am*" the God of Abraham, Isaac and Jacob though they had died hundreds of years before. If resurrection were not a fact He should have said, "I *was*" their God. The Lord also based a crucial argument concerning His own deity on the word *Lord* (Mt 22:41-46) as quoted from Psalm 110:1. If He did not consider the words of Scripture to be inerrant, the argument would have been meaningless. On another occasion He vindicated Himself from the charge of blasphemy by focusing on a single word in Psalm 82:6 (Jn 10:34). Then He enforced His argument by reminding His accusers that the Scripture cannot be broken. Paul, too, insisted on the importance of a singular in contrast to a plural in his argument in Galatians 3:16. Such an argument would be invalid unless the difference between singulars and plurals can be trusted. All of these examples force us to admit that the Bible claims inerrancy for itself.

5. No one who holds to inerrancy denies that the Bible uses ordinary figures of speech (like "corners of the earth," Rev 7:1), but they are accurately used.

6. Nor do we deny that authors sometimes researched their facts before writing (Lk 1:1-4). But the product, we believe, was kept from error by this superintending work of the Spirit.

7. Neither do we deny that there are problems in the text that we presently have. But problems are quite different from errors. Indeed, in the face of the claims that the Bible apparently makes for itself about inspiration and inerrancy, it would seem more reasonable when confronted with problems to place one's faith in the Scriptures which have been proved to be true again and again than in any fallible human opinion. Man's knowledge of these problems is limited and has in some instances been proved to be wrong. Time will undoubtedly continue to bring to light facts which will help solve the yet unsolved problems in the Bible.

WHAT BOOKS ARE IN THE BIBLE?

THE MEANING OF CANON

The question of which books belong in the Bible is called the question of the canon. The word *canon* means rule or measuring rod, and in relation to the Bible it refers to the collection of books which passed a test of authenticity and authority; it also means that those books are our rule of life. How was the collection made?

THE TESTS FOR CANONICITY

First of all it is important to remember that certain books were canonical even before any tests were put to them. That's like saying some students are intelligent before any tests are given to them. The tests only prove what is already intrinsically there. In the same way, neither the church nor councils made any book canonical or authentic; either the book was authentic or it was not when it was written. The church or its councils recognized and verified certain books as the Word of God, and in time those so recognized were collected together in what we now call the Bible.

What tests did the church apply?

1. There was the test of the authority of the writer. In relation to the Old Testament, this meant the authority of the lawgiver or the prophet or the leader in Israel. In relation to the New Testament, a book had to be written or backed by an apostle in order to be recognized. In other words, it had to have an apostolic signature or apostolic authorization. Peter, for instance, was the backer of Mark, and Paul of Luke.

2. The books themselves should give some internal evidences of their unique character, as inspired and authoritative. The content should commend itself to the reader as being different from an ordinary book in communicating the revelation of God.

3. The verdict of the churches as to the canonical nature of the books was important. There was in reality surprising unanimity among the early churches as to which books belonged in the inspired number. Although it is true that a few books were temporarily doubted by a minority, no book

whose authenticity was doubted by any large number of churches was later accepted.

THE FORMATION OF THE CANON

The canon of Scripture was, of course, being formed as each book was written, and it was complete when the last book was finished. When we speak of the "formation" of the canon we actually mean the recognition of the canonical books by the church. This took time. Some assert that all the books of the Old Testament canon were collected and recognized by Ezra in the fifth century B.C. References by Josephus (A.D. 95) and in 2 Esdras 14 (A.D. 100) indicate the extent of the Old Testament canon as the thirty-nine books we know. The discussions by the teaching-house at Jamnia (A.D. 70-100) seemed to assume this existing canon. Our Lord delimited the extent of the canonical books of the Old Testament when He accused the scribes of being guilty of slaying all the prophets God had sent Israel from Abel to Zacharias (Lk 11:51). The account of Abel's death is, of course, in Genesis; that of Zacharias is in 2 Chronicles 24:20-21, which is the last book in the order of the books in the Hebrew Bible (not Malachi as in our English Bibles). Therefore, it is as if the Lord had said, "Your guilt is recorded all through the Bible — from Genesis to Malachi." And He did not include any of the apocryphal books which were in existence at that time and which contained the accounts of other martyrs.

The first church council to list all twenty-seven books of the New Testament was the Council of Carthage in A.D. 397. Individual books of the New Testament were acknowledged as Scripture before this time (2 Pe 3:16; 1 Ti 5:17) and most were accepted in the era just after the apostles (Hebrews, James, 2 Peter, 2 and 3 John and Jude were debated for some time). The selection of the canon was a process that went on until each book proved its own worth by passing the tests for canonicity.

The twelve books of the Apocrypha were never accepted by the Jews or by our Lord on a par with the books of the Old Testament. They were revered but were not considered Scripture. The Septuagint (the Greek translation of the Old Testament done in the third century B.C.) included the Apocrypha with the Old Testament canonical books. Jerome (*c.* A.D. 340-420) in translating the Vulgate distinguished the canonical books from the ecclesiastical books (the Apocrypha), which had the effect of according them a secondary status. The Council of Trent (1548) recognized them as canonical, though the Reformers rejected this decree. In our English Bibles the Apocrypha was set apart in the Coverdale, Geneva, and King James versions. The first English Bible to exclude it entirely as a matter of policy was an Amsterdam edition of the Geneva Bible published in 1640, and the first English Bible printed in America (the Aitken Bible, 1782) omitted it.

Is Our Present Text Reliable?

The original copies of the Old Testament were written on leather or papyrus from the time of Moses (*c.* 1450 B.C.) to the time of Malachi (400 B.C.). Until the sensational discovery of the Dead Sea Scrolls in 1947 we did not possess copies of the Old Testament earlier than A.D. 895. The reason for this is simply that the Jews had an almost superstitious veneration for the text which impelled them to bury copies that had become too old for use. Indeed, the Masoretes (traditionalists) who between A.D. 600 and 950 added accents and vowel points and in general standardized the Hebrew text, devised complicated safeguards for the making of copies. They checked each copy carefully by counting the middle letter of pages, books and sections. Someone has said that everything countable was counted. When the Dead Sea Scrolls were discovered, they gave us a Hebrew text from the second to first century B.C. of all but one of the books (Esther) of the Old Testament. This was of the greatest importance, for it provided a much earlier check on the accuracy of the Masoretic text, which has now proved to be extremely accurate.

Other early checks on the Hebrew text include the Septuagint translation (middle of third century B.C.), the Aramaic Targums (paraphrases and quotes of the Old Testament), quotations in early Christian writers, and the Latin translation of Jerome (A.D. 400) which was made directly from the Hebrew text of his day. All of these give us the data for being assured of having an accurate text of the Old Testament.

More than 5,000 manuscripts of the New Testament exist today, which makes the New Testament the best-attested document in all ancient writings. The contrast is quite startling.

> Perhaps we can appreciate how wealthy the New Testament is in manuscript attestation if we compare the textual material for other ancient historical works. For Caesar's *Gallic War* (composed between 58 and 50 B.C.) there are several extant MSS, but only nine or ten are good, and the oldest is some 900 years later than Caesar's day. Of the 142 books of the Roman history of Livy (59 B.C.– A.D. 17), only 35 survive; these are known to us from not more than twenty MSS of any consequence, only one of which, and that containing fragments of Books III-VI, is as old as the fourth century. Of the fourteen books of the *Histories* of Tacitus (*c.* A.D. 100) only four and a half survive; of the sixteen books of his *Annals,* ten survive in full and two in part. The text of these extant portions of his two great historical works depends entirely on two MSS, one of the ninth century and one of the eleventh. . . . The History of Thucydides (*c.* 460-400 B.C.) is known to us from eight MSS, the earliest belonging to *c.* A.D. 900, and a few papyrus scraps, belonging to about the beginning of the Christian era. The same is true of the History of Herodotus (*c.* 480-425 B.C.). Yet no classical scholar would listen to an argument that the authenticity of Herodotus or

Thucydides is in doubt because the earliest MSS of their works which are of any use are over 1,300 years later than the originals.[2]

Not only are there so many copies of the New Testament in existence, but many of them are early. The approximately seventy-five papyri fragments date from A.D. 135 to the eighth century and cover parts of twenty-five of the twenty-seven books and about 40 percent of the text. The many hundreds of parchment copies include the great Codex Sinaiticus (4th century), the Codex Vaticanus (also 4th century), and the Codex Alexandrinus (5th century). In addition, there are 2,000 lectionaries (church service books containing many Scripture portions), more than 86,000 quotations of the New Testament in the church Fathers, old Latin, Syriac and Egyptian translations dating from the third century, and Jerome's Latin translation. All of this data plus all of the scholarly work that has been done with it assure us that we possess today an accurate and reliable text of the New Testament.

UNDERSTANDING THE BIBLE

A proper understanding of the Bible depends on two things: (1) the illuminating work of the Holy Spirit, and (2) the interpreting work of the reader.

ILLUMINATION

Although the word *illumination* has been applied to several aspects of doctrine (like the general enlightenment that the coming of Christ brought to all men, Jn 1:9, and the illumination theory of inspiration), it is generally thought of in connection with the ministry of the Holy Spirit which makes clear the truth of the written revelation in the Bible. In reference to the Bible, *revelation* relates to its content or material, *inspiration* to the method of recording that material, and *illumination* to the meaning of the record. The unsaved man cannot experience the illuminating ministry of the Spirit since he is blinded to the truth of God (1 Co 2: 14). This does not mean he cannot learn anything of the facts of the Bible, but he considers what he knows as foolishness.

On the other hand, the Christian has been promised this illumination of the text (Jn 16:12-15; 1 Co 2:9 – 3:2). Taking these two passages together, several facts emerge:

1. The most obvious is that the Spirit Himself is the Teacher, and His presence in the life of the believer is the guarantee of the effectiveness of this ministry.

2. The content of His teaching encompasses "all the truth" (the definite article is present in Jn 16:13). It specifically includes an understanding of prophecy ("things to come").   •

3. The purpose of the Spirit's illumination is to glorify Christ, not Himself.

4. Carnality in the believer can hinder and even nullify this ministry of the Spirit (1 Co 3:1-2).

INTERPRETATION

Illumination, though assured, does not always guarantee automatic understanding. As indicated above, the believer must be in fellowship with the Lord in order to experience this ministry. But also he must study, using the teachers God has given to the church (Ro 12:7) and the abilities and means at his own disposal.

The basic principle of interpretation is to interpret plainly. The word *literal* is avoided here because it creates connotations which have to be corrected. Plain, straightforward interpretation includes at least the following concepts:

1. To interpret plainly one must first of all understand what each word means in its normal grammatical historical sense.

2. Plain interpretation does not exclude the use of figures of speech. Indeed, a figure of speech may communicate more clearly, but what it communicates is plain. In other words, behind every figure of speech is a plain meaning, and that is what the interpreter seeks.

3. Always read with understanding the context in which a verse or passage appears, for this will throw light on its meaning. Beware, for instance, of the speaker who says, "Now you don't need to turn to this verse." He may be taking it out of its context and giving it another meaning. It is not only always safe but prudent to read what precedes and what follows.

4. Recognize the progress of revelation. Remember that the Bible was not handed down all at once as a complete book but that it came from God through many different writers over a period of about 1,600 years. This means that in the progress of revealing His message to man, God may add or even change in one era what He had given in another. The New Testament adds much that was not revealed in the Old. Furthermore, what God revealed as binding in one period may be rescinded in another (as the prohibition of eating pork, once binding on God's people, has been lifted today, 1 Ti 4:3). This is most important; otherwise, the Bible will contain apparently unresolvable contradictions (as Mt 10:5-7 compared with 28:18-20).

5. Expect the Bible to use what is technically called phenomenal language. This simply means that it often describes things as they appear to be rather than in precise scientific terms. Speaking of the sun rising or setting (neither of which it does) is an example of this (Mt 5:45; Mk 1:32), but this is a plain and normal way to communicate.

6. Recognize the important divisions of the Bible when interpreting it. The most basic is the difference between the Old and New Testaments. But there are also different kinds of writings — historical, poetic, prophetic — which must be recognized as different if they are to be inter-

preted correctly. Other landmarks in the Bible which affect proper interpretation are things like the great covenant made with Abraham (Gen 12:1-3), and the one with David (2 Sa 7), and the mystery of the church the body of Christ (Eph 3:6), and the difference between law and grace (Jn 1:17; Ro 6:14).

These suggestions are simply facets of the basic concept of plain interpretation. And that is the way God intended His inspired Bible to be understood.

3

Jesus Christ the Lord

THE UNIQUENESS of Christianity is the Person, Jesus Christ, and the distinctiveness of Christ is the fact that He is the God-man. In other words, He is a divine-human Being, something unique in time and eternity. It is also a concept very difficult to understand, for we have no basis for comparison with another God-man in history nor do we get any help from our experience. Yet this is not a dogma imposed on us simply to receive without question; it is a conclusion which grows out of the evidence in the Bible. Many facts point to the conclusion that Jesus Christ is God; many others lead to the conclusion that He is truly human; at the same time we see only one Person moving across the pages of the gospels. This union of undiminished deity and perfect humanity forever in one Person is called the doctrine of the hypostatic union (that is, the union of two hypostases or natures), and this is the uniqueness of Jesus Christ.

THE DEITY OF CHRIST

HIS PREEXISTENCE

Did Christ exist before He was born at Bethlehem? The answer is yes. While this does not of itself prove His deity (for He might, for instance, have existed as an angel before His birth), it certainly seems necessary to validate His claim to be the revelation of God and the Revealer of the Father. Did He exist before He was born? Names given to Him in the Old Testament indicate this. Micah 5:2 teaches the eternity of the Son, for the word translated "from of old" is used in Habakkuk 1:12 of God's eternal nature; thus, what God is, the Son is (see also Is 9:6). Furthermore, He Himself claimed to be preexistent, for He said, "Before Abraham [came to be], I am" (Jn 8:58). The statement, "I am," is not only a claim to existence before Abraham but also is a reference to the sacred name of God, *Yahweh*, and thus a claim to be God (Ex 3:14-15). Certain works which are said to have been done by Christ could only have been accomplished if He existed before time (e.g., creation, Col 1: 16). Of course, His claims to be God, which are discussed in the next section, include preexistence.

HIS DEITY

Many in our day deny the deity of Christ, knowing that in doing so they are undermining the central aspect of Christianity because they have removed from it the divine Saviour. This denial is not new, for even in the early church there were those who did so: Ebionites, dynamic Monarchians, and the Arians all denied that the Son possessed full deity. In the days of the Reformation, the Socinians followed their example and regarded Jesus as merely a man. Schleiermacher, Ritschl, Unitarians and liberals have done the same in more recent times. Today those who deny His full deity regard Jesus either as a great man (to be followed but not worshiped), a good man (who had the courage to die for His convictions), or a man more advanced than any other in His time. Along with such views of Christ goes a denial of the biblical accounts of His miraculous birth, death and resurrection.

Popularly, opponents of His deity assert that Jesus of Nazareth never claimed to be God. It was His followers, they say, who made that claim for Him, and, of course, they were mistaken. This is simply not so, for He did claim to be God, as we shall see. Obviously opponents of Christ's deity do not consider the Bible as authoritative but feel perfectly free to question statements of Scripture as to their reliability. Although denying the infallibility of the Bible does not always result in denying the deity of Christ, denying the deity of Christ must be accompanied by a denial of the accuracy of Scripture, for there is simply too much evidence in Scripture for His deity to do otherwise.

1. *His assertions.* Jesus of Nazareth claimed equality with God when He said that He and the Father were one (Jn 5:18; 10:30). Those who heard Him make this statement understood the force of such a claim, for they accused Him of blasphemy. If He were only claiming to be some kind of superman, they would not have bothered with the blasphemy charge. When Christ stood before the high priest, He gave a clear affirmative answer to the question whether He was the Christ (Mt 26:63-64). And His reply was given under oath.

In both John 10:36 and Matthew 26:63 the phrase "Son of God" is used, which some claim means something less than deity in order to avoid the conclusion that Christ claimed to be God. This is not so.

> In Jewish usage the term "son of . . ." did not generally imply any subordination, but rather equality and identity of nature. Thus Bar Kokba, who led the Jewish revolt 132-135 A.D. in the reign of Hadrian, was called by a name which means "Son of the Star." It is supposed that he took this name to identify himself as the very Star predicted in Numbers 24:17. The name Son of Consolation (Acts 4: 36) doubtless means, "The Consoler." "Sons of Thunder" (Mark 3:17) probably means "Thunderous Men." "Son of Man," especially as applied to Christ in Daniel 7:13 and constantly in the New Testament, essentially means "The Representative Man." Thus for Christ to say, "I am the Son of God" (John 10:36) was understood by His contemporaries as identifying Himself as God, equal with the Father, in an unqualified sense.[1]

Not only did Jesus make the claim to be equal with God for Himself, but the writers of the New Testament did the same. See John 1:1; 20:28; Romans 9:5; Philippians 2:6; Titus 2:13.

2. *His works.* Furthermore, Jesus of Nazareth claimed to do certain things which only God can do. In a classic confrontation with the scribes the Lord demonstrated He had the power to forgive sins by healing a man sick of the palsy. The scribes considered this claim to be blasphemy because they recognized that only God can forgive sins. The miracle of healing was done in order to validate Christ's claim to be able to forgive sins (Mk 2:1-12).

On other occasions He claimed that *all* judgment was given into His hands (Jn 5:27), that He would send the Holy Spirit (Jn 15:26), and that He would be the one to raise the dead (Jn 5:25). Since these are all prerogatives of deity, they substantiate His claim to be God or else they make Him a liar.

Elsewhere in the New Testament, works are attributed to Christ which only God can perform, further substantiating His equality with God. See John 1:3 and Colossians 1:16 for His work of creating, Colossians 1:17 and Hebrews 1:3 for the work of upholding all things, and Acts 17:31 for His being Judge of all men.

3. *His characteristics.* Jesus of Nazareth possessed characteristics which only God has. He claimed to be all-powerful (Mt 28:18; cf. Rev 1:8); He displayed knowledge that could only have come from His being omniscient (Mk 2:8; Jn 1:48); He made a promise which we often quote that depends on His being present everywhere (Mt 18:20; cf. Mt 28:20; Eph 1:23). These very distinctive claims indicate either that He was God or a great deceiver.

4. *His ascriptions.* Others ascribed to the Lord the prerogatives of deity in substantiation of His own claims. He was worshiped by men and by angels (Mt 14:33; Phil 2:10; Heb 1:6). His name is coupled with other Members of the Trinity in a relationship of equality (Mt 28:19; 2 Co 13:14). The writer to the Hebrews declared that He was

the same in substance with the Father — "the exact likeness of his substance" (Heb 1:3, free trans.). Coupled with Paul's statement that "in Him dwells all the fulness of deity in bodily form" (Col 2:9, free trans.), these are very strong declarations of His full deity equal with the deity of the Father and the Spirit. Too, He is called Yahweh in the New Testament, which could only be true if He were fully God. Notice Luke 1:76 compared with Malachi 3:1, and Romans 10:13 compared with Joel 2:32. Add other names of deity which He is given (God, Heb 1:8; Lord, Mt 22:43-45; King of kings and Lord of lords, Rev 19:16), and we can only conclude that Christ's deity is fully attested by the ascriptions given Him in the New Testament.

Remember that in each of these four lines of evidences for the deity of Christ, the proofs have been cited from two sources — the claims which the Lord Himself made as taken from His own words, and the claims which others made of Him in New Testament books other than the gospels. Both are equally valid, though there are some people today who deprecate the writers of the New Testament but who still pay some attention to Christ's own words. In helping people to acknowledge the evidence for the deity of our Lord it may be useful to keep this distinction in mind and present to them first Christ's own claims before presenting the evidence of the rest of the New Testament.

THE HUMANITY OF CHRIST

Jesus was not only fully God but also fully man — with one important exception to our usual concept of humanity. He was without sin and no other human being has that characteristic.

THE INCARNATION

The incarnation was the way in which Christ took on humanity. The word means "in flesh," and the method of the incarnation was the virgin birth. Though there has been

debate over the meaning of "virgin" in Isaiah 7:14, there
can be no question that the New Testament quotation of the
prophecy intends us to understand "virgin" (Mt 1:23). Furthermore, the use of a *feminine* relative *singular* pronoun in
Matthew 1:16 shows that the birth of Jesus was connected
exclusively with Mary and not Joseph. The Scriptures say
only that the Holy Spirit came upon Mary to generate the
child within her (Lk 1:35).

The New Testament states the following purposes for the
incarnation: to reveal God to men (Jn 1:18), to provide an
example for living (1 Pe 2:21), to provide a sacrifice for sin
(Heb 10:1-10), to destroy the works of the devil (1 Jn 3:8),
to enable Him to be a merciful and faithful High Priest
(Heb 5:1-2), to fulfill the promise of a son to sit on the
throne of David forever (Lk 1:31-33). Each of these purposes is worth considerable study, and we can only mention
the highlights here. As a man, He provides an example for
our lives. Only a man can die, so the Saviour had to become
incarnate in order to be able to die. Because He lived here
on earth as a man, He can understand and sympathize as our
Priest. Remember, however, that His humanity was always
perfect (Heb 4:15; 2 Co 5:21).

THE PROOFS OF HUMANITY

He had a human body. Although His conception was
supernatural, He did possess a human body, born as a baby
and developing as human beings do (Mt 1:18; Gal 4:4; Lk
2:52). He referred to Himself as a man and was recognized
by others as such (Jn 8:40; 1 Jn 1:1).

He had a human soul and spirit. It is important to remember that the *humanity* of Christ included body, soul
and spirit — material and immaterial. It was not that the
humanity provided only the body while the deity provided
the soul and spirit in the person of Christ. The humanity
was complete and therefore included both material and immaterial aspects (Mt 26:38; Lk 23:46).

He had the characteristics of a human being. Jesus was hungry (Mt 4:2), He was thirsty (Jn 19:28), He grew tired (Jn 4:6), He experienced love and compassion (Mt 9:36), He wept (Jn 11:35), and He was tested (Heb 4:15).

He possessed human names. He called Himself the Son of man, linking Himself to the work of Saviour and coming King (Lk 19:10). He was called the Son of David (Mk 10: 47), Jesus (Mt 1:21), and a man (1 Ti 2:5).

THE UNION OF DEITY AND HUMANITY OF CHRIST

How deity and humanity were united in the person of Jesus Christ has been debated hotly throughout church history. Everything that can be questioned about the proposition that Jesus Christ was one person with two natures, divine and human, has been questioned. Some have denied the deity of Christ (Ebionites, Arians). Others denied the reality of His humanity, feeling that He was simply a phantomlike appearance of God (Docetists). The Apollinarians claimed that the humanity was incomplete, the spirit being that of the eternal Logos. Others declared that He was adopted as divine at His baptism (Unitarians). Jehovah's Witnesses claim He was God's highest created representative. Barthians hold that He was fully human (including a sinful nature) and that God worked through this man to reveal Himself, especially at the cross.

Orthodoxy has always held that Jesus Christ was fully God and perfect man, and that these two natures were united in one person without forming a third nature (as Eutychius said) or two separate persons (as Nestorius taught).

THE KENOSIS OF CHRIST

The meaning of Philippians 2:1-11 has been greatly debated in relation to the person of the incarnate Christ. It is the connotation of the verb that appears in verse 7 that is disputed (*kenoō*, from which comes the name of this doc-

trine, *kenosis,* translated "made himself of no reputation" in
the AV and "emptied himself" in the RSV). Simply stated,
the question is, Did Christ empty Himself of some or all
aspects of deity when He came to earth?

That He possessed the attributes of deity before the incarnation is stated in verse 6, for He continued to subsist in the
form of God (the participle *huparchon* having this meaning). Indeed, it seems to say that even during the incarnation He continued to subsist in the form of God. The word
"form" means not external accidents but essential attributes of deity. He did not merely appear as God; He was
God. "Form of God" must have as much reality as the parallel phrase, "form of a servant" in verse 7. If He was really a
servant (human being), as those who deny His deity are
quite happy to admit, then He was also really God. You
cannot have the reality of one without the reality of the
other, according to this passage.

But in what sense does Paul mean that Christ emptied
Himself at the incarnation? "Emptied" may be a misleading
translation because it connotes Christ's giving up or losing
some of His divine attributes during His earthly life, and
that was not the case. Therefore, the kenosis cannot be
understood to mean a subtraction of deity but the addition
of humanity with its consequent limitations. Indeed, in the
passage itself, the verb "emptied" is explained by three participles which follow — (1) taking the form of a servant,
(2) becoming in the likeness of men, and (3) being found
in fashion as a man. The kenosis is further explained in the
text by the parallel clause which follows, "He humbled himself." The idea is that by taking on humanity with its limitations, there was a humbling which, although real, did not
involve the giving up of any divine attributes.

If our Lord did surrender some of His divine attributes
when He came to earth, then His essential character would
have been changed, and He would not have been fully God
while on earth. You cannot subtract any attributes without

changing the character of the person. Often those who do subtract take away the omni attributes (omniscience, omnipotence, omnipresence), but we have already seen in the section on the deity of Christ that He possessed these particular attributes during the period of His incarnation (Mt 28:18; 18:20; Mk 2:8). Thus any doctrine of kenosis which says Christ surrendered attributes at the incarnation is in direct conflict with scriptural evidence concerning His person during the incarnation.

What is included in a proper statement of the true doctrine of the kenosis? The concept involves the veiling of Christ's preincarnate glory (Jn 17:5), the condescension of taking on Himself the likeness of sinful flesh (Ro 8:3), and the voluntary nonuse of some of His attributes of deity during the time of His earthly life (Mt 24:36). His humanity was not a glorified humanity and was thus subject to temptation, weakness, pain and sorrow. Choosing not to use His divine attributes is quite different from saying that He gave them up. Nonuse does not mean subtraction.

THE IMPECCABILITY OF CHRIST

The meaning of *impeccability* has also been debated. Some, of course, do not think Christ was sinless, but among those who do there are two views of impeccability. One says that He was able not to sin while the other states that He was not able to sin. In either case He did not sin, though one viewpoint involves the possibility that He could have. That idea is usually held because it is hard to understand how His temptations could have been real if He could not have sinned. That He did not sin and that He was tempted are facts agreed on. How could the temptations have been real if He could not have sinned?

Part of the answer lies in discovering what Hebrews 4:15 says and what it does not say. Literally, the verse reads this way: " . . . having been tested according to all, according to likeness, apart from sin." It does not say that Christ was

tempted with a view to succumbing to sin. He was tested
with a view to proving He was sinless. It does not say that
He was tested in every particular specific test that man can
be put to. It does say that His tests were in all the areas in
which a man can be tested: the lust of the flesh, the lust of
the eyes, and the pride of life. The particular tests within
those areas were entirely different for Him from the ones for
us. The phrase "according to likeness" apparently means
that He could be tested because He took the likeness of sinful flesh. "Apart from sin" means that, having no sin nature,
He could not have been tested from that avenue, as we can
and usually are.

His temptations were really not to see if He could sin, but
to prove that He could not. Nevertheless, they were real, for
the reality of a test does not lie either in the moral nature of
the one tested or in the ability to yield to it. And, of course,
His ability to sympathize with us does not demand a one-to-
one correspondence in the particulars of the tests.

THE EARTHLY LIFE OF CHRIST

THE EVENTS OF HIS LIFE

The earthly life of Christ is doctrinally important for several reasons. First, it proved the validity of His claims and
thus His worthiness to be the Saviour. It was the time when
the Lamb was tested and proved to be a proper sacrifice for
sin. Second, His earthly life furnishes an example for His
people to follow. This particularly means the example of His
self-sacrificing love (1 Jn 2:6). Third, it was during His
earthly life that His teachings were given. Some of those
teachings concerned the Jewish people directly, and some
were given in anticipation of the founding of His church.

The life of Christ may be divided into three parts. First,
there were the years of preparation beginning with His
birth in Bethlehem, through the years of infancy, childhood
and growth into full manhood, and concluding with His bap-

tism and temptation. Second, there followed the years of public ministry which included His early ministry in Judea (Jn 2:13–4:3), His ministry in Galilee (Mk 1:14–9:50), and the Perean ministry (Lk 9:51–19:28). Third, there were events leading up to His death and the crucifixion itself. These occurred during what is called Passion Week (Lk 19:29–22:46) and included the betrayal and arrest (Jn 18:2-13), the trial before Annas (Jn 18:12-24), the trial before Caiaphas (Mk 14:53–15:1), the first trial before Pilate (Mk 15:1-5), the trial before Herod (Lk 23:8-12), the second trial before Pilate (Mk 15:6-15), and the crucifixion itself with its various words spoken from the cross. Further details of His life may be found in any standard life of Christ, and the doctrinal significance of His death is studied in chapter 8.

THE OFFICES HE OCCUPIED

During His life the Lord occupied and exercised the three offices of prophet, priest and king.

The prophet was the channel through which God's message was delivered to man. Our Lord called Himself a prophet (Mt 13:57) and was undoubtedly the greatest of all prophets, for He not only delivered God's message to man, but He also revealed God in His life and person. Of all His teachings only a portion have been recorded, but the scope and comprehensiveness of the revelation that came through Christ are beyond any other. Three lengthy and important discourses should be studied – the Sermon on the Mount (Mt 5–7), the Olivet discourse (Mt 24–25), and the upper room discourse (Jn 13–16).

Our Lord was a priest after the order of Melchisedec although He performed many of the functions that were illustrated by the Aaronic priests. He was appointed by God, fully qualified, offered a sacrifice for sin, and represented His people before God (Heb 5:1-10). Of course His priestly ministry in behalf of believers continues today in His interceding for us and His sustaining us (Heb 7:25; Rev 2:1).

The office of Christ as King was predicted before His birth (Is 9:6-7, Lk 1:31-33). When He came He fulfilled the requirements of that promised King although His people rejected His claims. The result of that rejection was not an annulment of the kingdom promises, but simply a delay in their fulfillment until the second advent of the King. In the meantime He is building His church. The delay in no way puts in doubt the certainty of future fulfillment nor does it alter the fact that He always is King in His person.

> Taken together, the three offices of Christ as Prophet, Priest and King are the key to the purpose of the incarnation. His prophetic office was concerned with the revelation of the truth of God; the priestly office was related to His work as Saviour and Mediator; His kingly office had in view His right to reign over Israel and over the entire earth. In Christ the supreme dignity of these offices is reached.[2]

THE RESURRECTION AND ASCENSION OF CHRIST

THE FACT OF THE RESURRECTION

The fact of the bodily resurrection of Christ is overwhelmingly attested to in the Bible. First of all, man is confronted with an empty tomb. Many explanations are offered as to why it was empty, but they are all unbelievable except the one that says He arose from the dead. To say that the disciples went to the wrong tomb and happened to find one that was empty requires a lot of faith, since there were Roman soldiers and angels stationed at Christ's tomb, making it rather easy to find. To say that the body was stolen by outside parties was known to be a fabrication in those days (Mt 28:11-15). If it had been stolen then why was it not produced the moment the disciples began to preach the bodily resurrection of Christ from the dead? That would have silenced their preaching quickly and completely. To say that the disciples stole the body is to conclude that they were willing to die as martyrs for something they knew to be a lie. Furthermore, the orderly condition in which the graveclothes were found by those who came to the tomb indicates that the body was not stolen. Robbers would not have un-wrapped the body in the first place; but if they did, they certainly would have left the wrappings in disarray (Jn 20:6-7). The empty tomb is impossible to explain apart from bodily resurrection.

Second, all the appearances of the Lord after the resurrection are evidence that He did rise, and those appearances came at various times, to various people and under various circumstances — all of which indicate that they were not staged (Jn 20:11-17; Mt 28:9-10; 1 Co 15:5; Lk 24:13-35, 36-43; Jn 20:26-29; 21:1-23; 1 Co 15:6). The sheer number of witnesses to the appearances of Christ after the resurrection makes it impossible to conceive of the story being fabricated by a few.

Third, many subsequent events of history also attest to the resurrection. For example, on the day of Pentecost, Peter declared that Jesus had been raised less than two months before in the same city where he was preaching, and he was not challenged or contradicted. Indeed, his message was believed by 3,000 people. The very marked change in Peter and the others, the growth of the church, and the beginning of worship on Sunday all are results of the resurrection.

THE NATURE OF THE RESURRECTION

Christ rose bodily from the dead. His was not a resurrection of "influence" or "spirit." The resurrection does not mean simply that His memory lives on, but it was a physical, bodily resurrection. Those bodily characteristics of His resurrection body were felt and seen by the disciples (Lk 24:39; Jn 20:27), and He demonstrated certain physical functions when He ate with them (Lk 24:42-43). His resurrection body was clearly identified with the same one which was crucified and buried.

But it was also different in that it was not subject to normal limitations. For instance, ·after the resurrection He could pass through closed doors (Jn 20:19), but most important He cannot die ever again (Ro 6:9).

THE SIGNIFICANCE OF THE RESURRECTION

The resurrection proved the validity of Christ's claims about Himself and the truth of all that He said. The angel emphasized this at the open tomb (Mt 28:6) and Peter reiterated it on the day of Pentecost (Ac 2:30-31).

The resurrection is the everlasting guarantee of the forgiveness of our sins (1 Co 15:17). Our trust is not in myths or self-induced beliefs, but in the true and proven facts of the gospel.

The resurrection is also the guarantee of the certainty of future resurrection of all men — those who believe to everlasting life and those who do not believe to everlasting condemnation (Jn 5:28-29). Future judgment is also certain because the Judge has been raised from the dead (Ac 17:31).

The resurrection also has significance in relation to the life of the believer in providing power for his service and relationship to his risen Head (Eph 1:19-22), and assuring him of a sympathetic High Priest (Heb 4:14-16).

THE IMPORTANCE OF THE ASCENSION

Our Lord also predicted His ascension and exaltation (Jn 6:62; 17:1) which was fulfilled forty days after His resurrection (Ac 1:9-11).

The significance of the ascension includes the following: (1) It marked the conclusion of the period of His humiliation and limitation on earth. (2) It marked the beginning of the period of His exaltation at the right hand of the Father (Eph 1:20-23). (3) As Forerunner, it made Him the anchor for our faith (Heb 6:20). (4) It marked the beginning of His present ministries of being our High Priest and of preparing a place for our future abode (Heb 4:14-16; Jn 14:2). (5) It gave Him headship over the church and is especially related to His giving gifts to His body (Col 1:18; Eph 4:8).

THE PRESENT MINISTRY OF CHRIST

The present ministry of our Lord is chiefly related to His people in contrast to the present work of the Spirit which includes ministries to unbelievers, like enlightening and regenerating. Among the particulars of Christ's ministry are the following:

1. The risen and ascended Christ is praying for His people. This has several benefits: it guarantees the security of their salvation (Heb 7:25); it assures continued fellowship in the family of God (1 Jn 2:1); and it is a powerful preventive against sin in their lives (Jn 17:15).

2. The Lord is preparing a place for our everlasting habitation (Jn 14:3). He is anticipating the day when He will take us to be with Himself by preparing for our arrival in heaven.

3. Christ is now building the church which is His body (Mt 16:18).

4. The Head of the church is engaged in various activities on behalf of the members of His body. We have already noted that as ascended Head He gives gifts to men (Eph 4:11). These are essential to the proper functioning of the body. Furthermore, He indwells every member of the body of Christ (Gal 2:20). He Himself indwells us and He has sent the Spirit who also indwells us. The standard against which His indwelling power is measured is His own resurrection and ascension (Eph 1:18-20). The resurrection guarantees that His power can bring victory out of defeat, and His being seated at the right hand of the Father assures us that

His power can bring honor in place of dishonor. Too, the Lord is nurturing and cherishing the body of Christ (Eph 5:29). The idea in these words is that our Lord is fostering with tender concern the growth of His people. As Head He also gives union and direction to the church (Eph 2:20-21).

5. The Lord is also engaged in answering our prayers (Jn 14:14). When we pray in His name He will answer and the result will be even greater works than He did while on earth (Jn 14:12). This means greater in scope (worldwide now) and greater in kind (involving all the spiritual benefits which the coming of the Spirit unleashes).

6. He gives special help for particular needs (Heb 4:16). The help is promised just at the particular time that the need arises, according to this verse. This includes help (same Greek word) in times of temptation (Heb 2:18).

7. He is concerned with the fruitfulness of His followers (Jn 15:1-16).

Of course, none of these ministries would be operative if Christ were not alive today!

THE FUTURE MINISTRY OF CHRIST

The future ministries of our Lord include His coming for His own in the rapture of the church (1 Th 4:13-18), the pouring out of the wrath of the Lamb on the earth during the tribulation period (Rev 6:16-17), the return of the King of kings and Lord of lords to rule the world with a rod of iron (Rev 19:11-16), and His everlasting reign, first over the millennial kingdom, and then forever. These subjects are studied in detail in chapter 9.

4

The Holy Spirit

UNDOUBTEDLY the least understood Person of the Godhead is the Holy Spirit. As proof, just notice the difficult words in the preceding sentence. "Person" — what does that mean when speaking of three Persons yet one God? "Godhead" — why add the "-head"? And "Spirit" seems a strange word to use of a person. Yet a proper understanding of the Spirit is basic to many doctrines — inspiration of the Bible, several important aspects of salvation, and many facets of the Christian life. We start at the logical beginning by asking a question.

IS THE HOLY SPIRIT REALLY A PERSON?

When we use the word *person* we inevitably think first of human beings, so we naturally expect a person to be like a human being with a body as well as something immaterial which we call soul or spirit. We also speak of a person dying when we should actually say that his body died. In other words, everything is against our thinking of a person apart from a body. And, yet, we recognize that when a person dies, that individual has not ceased to exist; for his soul and spirit are either in heaven or hell. The body dies and the person continues to exist consciously. If you have a saved father or mother, for instance, who is dead, you know that he or she is alive in the presence of God. Therefore, we ought to be able to think of a person apart from a human body. Likewise, we know that angels exist as real beings, yet they do not have human bodies and they are called spirits. They are spirit personalities. And God Himself is spirit and a person. Thus if we could show that the Holy Spirit has

67

similar characteristics as persons do, then we would conclude that He too is really a person.

What constitutes the essentials of personality? Usually, three things — a person must possess intelligence, emotions, and will. A thing lacks these, but the Holy Spirit is not a thing because He has intelligence, emotions and will.

1. The Spirit is said to know the things of God, and that takes some intelligence (1 Co 2:10-11). We also read about "the mind of the Spirit" (Ro 8:27).

2. It is possible to grieve the Spirit (Eph 4:30), which is rather hard to conceive of doing to an influence or thing!

3. It is the Spirit who distributes spiritual gifts "as he wills" (1 Co 12:11). The phrase might even be translated "as he purposes," because it shows a definite act of the will.

Thus, the Spirit does possess the characteristics of a person.

Although the Spirit does many things which are performed by people, not all of them are exclusively the activities of people. For instance, the Spirit teaches, but so do circumstances. We learn from experiences but that does not mean that experiences are persons. However, there are some things which the Spirit does which *only persons* can do. For instance, He prays for us (Ro 8:26). Things and influences don't pray. He also performs miracles (Ac 8:39) — something only persons can do.

The Greek word for spirit is *pneuma* (from which we derive words that have to do with air, like *pneumatic* or *pneumonia*), and it is a neuter gender word. Proper grammar teaches us that when a pronoun is substituted for a noun it must be of the same gender as the noun, but this is not always the case when pronouns are substituted for the word *Spirit*. In John 16:13-14, for instance, the pronoun "he" ("howbeit when he" and "he shall glorify me") is masculine. The same happens in Ephesians 1:14 where the word translated *which* is actually a masculine pronoun *who*. These are instances of bad grammar but excellent theology, for they show that the Spirit is not a neuter thing but a definite person.

YES, BECAUSE HE IS RELATED TO OTHERS AS A PERSON

How, for example, could you reasonably interpret the baptismal formula ("in the name of the Father, and of the Son, and of the Holy Spirit," Mt 28:19) as referring to two persons (Father and Son) and one thing (Holy Spirit)? Too, the Spirit is related to the Lord in such a way as to conclude that both are persons (Jn 16:14). Once He is related to human beings in a manner that would make it very unnatural to conclude anything other than that He is a person (Ac 15:28).

THOSE WHO HAVE SAID HE IS NOT A PERSON

A modalistic concept of the Trinity has been the chief reason for denying either the personality or deity of the Spirit through its various forms throughout the centuries. Sabellianism (A.D. 215) taught that God is a unity and that He revealed Himself in three different modes of forms. God played three roles. This error denied the distinct personality of the Spirit. Socinianism (1539-1604) defined the Spirit as "virture or energy flowing from God to man." Most liberal theology today agrees with this; and although the Spirit is mentioned often, He is no person, only a power or influence. Barthianism has often been accused of modalism; and while some would reject this, it nevertheless is probably an accurate description of the Barthian view of the Trinity.

Is the Holy Spirit Completely God?

The proof of the personality of the Spirit does not, of course, include the proof that He is God. The reverse is true, however, for if He is God He must also be a person as God is. The denial of deity and personality usually go together, though some believe He is a person without believing that He is also divine.

YES, BECAUSE HE HAS CHARACTERISTICS POSSESSED ONLY BY GOD

1. The Spirit, we are told, knows the things of God in a way in which man does not and in a way which implies His omniscience — an attribute which only God possesses (1 Co 2:11-12).

2. Further, no one can escape the presence of the Spirit wherever He might try to go, and omnipresence is an attribute only God has (Ps 139:7).

YES, BECAUSE HE DID THINGS WHICH ONLY GOD CAN DO

Some of the works which only God can do and which the Holy Spirit does (and which, therefore, show that He must be God) are: (1) regeneration (causing a person to be born again, Jn 3:5-6), (2) begetting the humanity of Jesus Christ (Lk 1:35), (3) the creation of the world (Ps 104:30).

YES, BECAUSE HE IS ASSOCIATED ON AN EQUAL PLANE WITH THE OTHER PERSONS OF THE TRINITY

One of the strongest proofs of the deity of the Spirit is the identification of the Spirit with Yahweh of the Old Testament. This is seen in passages where the Old Testament records that Yahweh said something and the New Testament quotation of that same passage is attributed to the Spirit as the Speaker. That would seem to say very clearly that the Spirit, like Yahweh, is fully divine (Is 6:1-13 and Ac 28:25; Jer 31:31-34 and Heb 10:15-17).

In the New Testament, blasphemy of and lying to the Holy Spirit are the same as if done to God (Mt 12:31-32; Ac 5:

3-4). Also the Spirit is associated equally with the other Members of the Godhead in the baptismal formula (Mt 28:19) and in the benediction of 2 Corinthians 13:14. All these instances argue for His being a true person.

PROCESSION

Procession is a term which has been used by theologians to try to describe the relationship between the Spirit and the other Persons of the Trinity. It does not imply any sort of inequality, as if the Spirit were less in deity than the Father and the Son, but it is supposed to express a subordination of relationship. John 15:26 is the scriptural basis for the concept, and it was stated in a formal way in the Constantinopolitan Creed (381). Some at that time had begun to deny the full deity of the Spirit and to maintain that the Spirit was a creature who was subordinate to the Son. The group that did this were called the Macedonians (after their founder, Macedonius) and nicknamed Pneumatomachians ("evil speakers against the Spirit"). A council was called and it formulated this statement: "And we believe in the Holy Spirit, the Lord, the Life-giving, who proceeds from the Father, who is to be glorified with the Father and the Son, and who speaks through the prophets." Although the statement did not call the Spirit God, it did counter the Macedonians, because what it ascribed to the Spirit could not be true of any creature. In 451 the Council of Chalcedon confirmed the decision of Constantinople and firmly established the doctrine of the deity of the Spirit.

However, in 589 the Synod of Toledo, attempting to probe further the mysterious question of the Spirit's relation to the other Persons of the Trinity, felt that Constantinople's statement that the Spirit proceeded from the Father might seem to be a denial of the oneness of the Son with the Father. Therefore, they added the famous *filioque* clause (the Spirit proceeds from the Father *and the Son*). The Western church continued to repeat the clause in subsequent creeds; but the

Eastern church rejected it on the ground that it implied the Spirit was not fully divine, and that branch of the church continues to consider it heresy.

These historical debates may seem a bit useless, but there is profit in reviewing them because in the process we force ourselves to think about these important matters concerning deity, equality, subordination and relationship. And in so doing it will perhaps help us to be more careful in how we talk about these matters. The study of doctrine should not only help us understand the truth but it should also help us to express it in the very best and clearest way because we have thought about it carefully. Looking over the shoulders of the ancients and listening in on their discussions are of great help in doing this.

THE WORK OF THE SPIRIT IN THE OLD TESTAMENT

HIS PART IN CREATION

Sometimes in the Old Testament it is not always clear whether a reference which uses the word *spirit* is referring to the Holy Spirit or, for instance, to the breath of God's own mouth (see Ps 33:6). Nevertheless, there are indications from specific references that the Holy Spirit did have a part in the work of creation. In addition, the fact that He is God and as God is immanent (present) in the world would involve Him in all the works of God, including creation.

Particularly, the Spirit's part was related to giving the creation life (Ps 104:30; Job 33:4), order (Is 40:12-13; Job 26:13), adornment to the glory of God (Ps 33:6; Job 26:13), and continual renewing or preservation (an aspect usually associated with Christ, though in Ps 104:29-30 related to the Spirit).

HIS PART IN REVELATION

In chapter 2 some matters related to revelation and inspiration were discussed, so we need here only to delineate the Spirit's particular work in this area.

The chief human instrument that God used in the Old Testament to give His message to man was the prophet, but behind him was the Holy Spirit moving and guiding so that the writer communicated exactly what God wanted man to know. Referring to the Old Testament writers, Peter said that "men spake from God, being moved by the Holy Spirit" (2 Pe 1:21, ASV). This general statement is supported by many specific examples (2 Sa 23:2; Mic 3:8). In addition, the New Testament directly attributes many Old Testament Scripture verses to the Spirit (Mt 22:43; Ac 1:16; 4:25). Concerning the New Testament, the Lord promised that the Spirit would recall to the apostles' minds the things which He had taught them (Jn 14:26). Thus the Spirit was the single Author guiding and guarding the revelation; the instruments or agents were men, and the ultimate source was God.

HIS RELATION TO MAN

Selective (though not necessarily permanent) indwelling. The Bible declares that the Spirit was *in* certain Old Testament people, so there can be no question but that He did indwell in those days (Gen 41:38; Num 27:18; Dan 4:8; 1 Pe 1:11). But sometimes the Spirit is said to have come *upon* Old Testament people (Judg 3:10; 1 Sa 10:9-10). Is there any difference between being in and coming upon? Probably only that "coming upon" may indicate the possibility of going away as well (cf. Judg 15:14 with Judg 16:20). When the Lord contrasted the relationship of the Spirit to Old Testament men and those living after the day of Pentecost, He said that the Spirit had been abiding with them and that He would be in them (Jn 14:17). This seems definitely to indicate a difference in the pre- and post-Pentecost relationships, though the word *abides* shows that His ministry was not an erratic one in Old Testament times. Today all believers are permanently indwelt. This universality and permanency were apparently not guaranteed in Old Testament days.

Enablement for special service. The Spirit's special empowerment was for particular tasks like the construction of the tabernacle (Ex 31:3) as well as for other mighty works (Judg 14:6; 1 Sa 16:13).

General restraint of sin. Restraint was apparently His special work from the earliest times (Gen 6:3), and it is also possible that His very names and titles had a restraining effect on men as they thought about Him (Neh 9:20; Ps 51:11).

The Work of the Spirit in the Life of Christ

IN THE VIRGIN BIRTH

Gabriel told Mary plainly that the baby to be born to her would be conceived by the Holy Spirit (Lk 1:35), and Joseph was informed of the same fact by an angel (Mt 1:20).

IN HIS LIFE

Christ was anointed by the Spirit in some special way at the time of His baptism (Lk 4:18; Jn 1:32). This empowered Him for service for God (Ac 10:38). Our Lord was also filled with and led by the Spirit (Lk 4:1; see also Jn 3:34; Is 42:1) and He was empowered by the Spirit to do miracles (Mt 12:28). The obvious fact that Christ depended on the power of the Spirit illuminates the depth of His condescension, and it is a sharp reminder of our need of the Spirit's power as we live our lives on earth. If He depended, how much more must we?

IN HIS DEATH AND RESURRECTION

If Hebrews 9:14 refers to the Holy Spirit (and not to Christ's own spirit as some believe), then He offered Himself as a sacrifice through the Spirit. Romans 1:4 (and some think 1 Pe 3:18) may refer to the Spirit's work in His resurrection. Too, He gave commandments to the apostles and through them to us by the Spirit (Ac 1:2).

THE WORK OF THE SPIRIT IN SALVATION

Without question, one of the most important and largest areas of the Spirit's work today is in relation to salvation. Indeed, it is primarily His work from the beginning of conviction to the final delivery of that person in heaven.

CONVICTING (JN 16:8-11)

The idea of "conviction" is complex. It involves the conceptions of authoritative examination, of unquestionable proof, of decisive judgment, of punitive power. Whatever the final issue may be, he who "convicts" another places the truth of the case in dispute in a clear light before him, so that it must be seen and acknowledged as truth. He who then rejects the conclusion which the exposition involves, rejects it with his eyes open and at his peril. Truth seen as truth carries with it condemnation to all who refuse to welcome it.[1]

Thus the convicting work of the Spirit is the placing of the truth of the gospel in a clear light before the unsaved person so he acknowledges it as truth *whether or not he receives Christ as personal Saviour.* Conviction is making the message clear, not the saving of the soul — that's regeneration. In other words, the one who testifies about the saving grace of God must depend on the Spirit even to make that testimony understood clearly.

What truth is it that He makes clear? It is the truth about sin, righteousness and judgment (Jn 16:8 ff.). The proof that men are in a state of sin is because "they believe not on me." The righteousness of Christ is proved because of His resurrection from the dead and ascension to the Father. All of His righteous claims were fully vindicated when He returned to heaven. The proof of judgment to come is based on the past judgment of Satan. In other words, if Satan, Christ's archenemy, has been judged (Jn 12:31), what chance can any man hope to have of escaping judgment if he refuses the grace of God?

The order of the Spirit's work of conviction is a logical one. Man needs first to see his state of sin, then he needs to have proof of the righteousness of the Saviour who can save him from that sin, and finally he needs to be reminded that if he refuses to receive the Saviour he will face certain judgment and condemnation.

REGENERATING (TITUS 3:5)

Although the word *regeneration* is used only twice in the Bible (Titus 3:5, where it refers to the new birth, and Mt 19:28 where it refers to the millennial kingdom), the concept of being born again is found in other passages, notably John 3. Technically, it is God's act of begetting eternal life in the one who believes in Christ. While faith and regeneration are closely associated, the two ideas are distinct, faith being the human responsibility and the channel through which God's grace is received, and regeneration being God's supernatural act of imparting eternal life. The two must happen together, and any attempt to place one chronologically before the other cannot be more than useless academic exercise. Some argue that since a man dead in trespasses and sins cannot believe, God must first regenerate him in order that he may then believe. But, if that were true, that is, if he already had been regenerated and thus been given the gift of eternal life, then why would he need to believe? The two must be simultaneous. The Word of God is also closely associated with regeneration as the necessary revelation to give proper content to a man's faith (1 Pe 1:23; Ja 1:18).

Although the antecedents and consequences of regeneration involve processes in time, the act of regeneration itself is instantaneous. One is either unborn or born, and that great change happens in a moment of time. An individual may not know precisely the moment of his salvation, but in God's sight he is either dead in sins or born into the family of God. Regeneration brings with it a new nature (2 Co 5:17), which means a new capacity to serve righteousness. The old nature is not eradicated, for the capacity to serve self continues until we die. Regeneration does not make a man perfect, but it places him in the family of God and gives him the new ability to please his Father by growing into the image of Christ. Fruit from the new nature is proof that regeneration has occurred (1 Jn 2:29).

INDWELLING (1 CO 6:19)

The distinctive feature of the ministry of the Spirit today is His indwelling *every* believer, regardless of his spiritual condition. The easiest test of this is to notice that in the New Testament, sinning Christians are said to be indwelt. Remember the Corinthians? If ever there was a group of carnal believers, it was at Corinth (1 Co 3:3) — one brother (note 1 Co 5:5*b*) was living in gross sin, and many were at legal swords' points with each other (1 Co 6). And yet Paul says, without making any exceptions, that the Holy Spirit lived within their bodies (1 Co 6:19). Indeed, this is the basis for his exhortation not to defile their bodies. Furthermore, Romans 8:9 makes it clear that the absence of the Spirit is an evidence of an unsaved condition; therefore, if the Spirit were to come and go in a person's life, then he would have, lose, regain, lose, etc., his salvation.

How can a believer know that the Spirit of God is within Him? There are two avenues of assuring evidence. One is simply to believe the Word of God which says this is true. The other is to look at one's Christian experience as an evidence of the Spirit's presence and working in one's life. However, experience may not always be convincing since sin may hinder His work, and in the normal process of Christian development one's growth will be slow but steady with no unusual demonstrations of the power of God. This unspectacular kind of progress should never be diagnosed as indicating the absence of the indwelling Spirit. He does abide forever in every believer's life (Jn 14:16-17).

BAPTIZING (1 CO 12:13)

To many the word *baptism* conjurs up visions of water or spectacular displays of power. Neither is correct when speaking of the baptizing work of the Spirit. This is something entirely different from the ordinance of water baptism, and it is something which gives the Christian primarily a position and, only secondarily, power. Too, people often confuse baptism and the filling of the Spirit, but these are separate and distinct ministries of the Spirit. Some characteristics of the baptism of the Spirit are:

1. It is for all believers without exception. Again, it was to that carnal Corinthian church that Paul said all were baptized (1 Co 12:13). Notice, too, that he did not exhort them to be baptized as the way out of their carnality.

2. It occurred for the first time on the day of Pentecost (for it was still future when the Lord spoke of it in Ac 1:5, and Peter referred to it as happening first at Pentecost in Ac 11:15-16). Therefore, it is something distinct to this dispensation.

3. Apparently each believer is baptized only once (the tense of the verb in 1 Co 12:13 indicates an unrepeated experience).

4. It joins believers to the body of Christ and sets up a relationship from which all kinds of power and experiences can flow (Ro 6:1-10). However, the absence of unusual experiences does not indicate an unbaptized position (otherwise one could be a believer and *not* be in the body of Christ!). The carnal Corinthians had been baptized. The baptized Galatians were turning away from the true gospel (Gal 1:6; 3:27). Many were baptized who did not speak in tongues (1 Co 12:13, 30). To experience fully the benefits

of the new position which the baptism gives us involves the filling of the Spirit as well. But the baptism is basic to all Christian growth and experience.

SEALING (EPH 4:30)

One of the greatest assurances of the eternal security of the believer is the fact that the Father has sealed every believer with the Holy Spirit (2 Co 1:22; Eph 1:13; 4:30). All are sealed (including the carnal Corinthians!), and it occurs when we believe (Eph 1:13 should be translated "in whom having believed ye were sealed with that Holy Spirit of promise").

The concept of sealing includes the ideas of ownership, authority and security. Since God has sealed us, we are His possession, secure (unless there were someone with greater power than God Himself!) until the day of redemption. One of the best illustrations of sealing is registered mail. When something is registered at the post office, it is sealed until delivered and only two persons can open it — the sender or the recipient. In our case, God is both sender and recipient, so only God could break that seal; and He has promised to deliver us safely to heaven. That's eternal security in the clearest terms. But, notice the context of Ephesians 4:30. Sealing is the basis for an exhortation not to grieve the Spirit by committing sins, especially with the tongue. A proper understanding of security never breeds license.

THE WORK OF THE SPIRIT IN THE LIFE OF THE CHRISTIAN

HE GIVES GIFTS

The source of spiritual gifts. Spiritual gifts are given by the Holy Spirit sovereignly ("as he will," 1 Co 12:11) and specifically (1 Co 12:8-10).

The meaning of spiritual gifts. A spiritual gift is a God-given ability for service. If we keep in mind that a gift is primarily an ability, it will keep us from much of the confusion which exists in people's minds concerning gifts. Many

think of a spiritual gift as an office in the church which only
a privileged few can ever occupy. The gift of pastor, for instance, is usually associated with the office or position a person has in the pastorate. But in reality the gift is the ability
to give shepherdlike care to people, regardless of where this
is done. Neither is a gift a particular geographical or structured place of ministry. Teaching, for instance, can be done
anywhere in the world and in or out of the formal classroom
situation. It is the ability to communicate God's truth. Neither is a gift a specialized procedure or ministry to a particular age group. There is no gift of young people's work, nor is
there a gift of writing. These are techniques or procedures
by which spiritual gifts are ministered, but the gift is the
God-given ability.

The distribution of spiritual gifts. We have already noticed
that spiritual gifts are given by the Spirit according to His
sovereign will. Apparently every Christian does (or at least
can) have some gifts (1 Pe 4:10), but this does not mean
that any single believer (nor necessarily any congregation)
has all the gifts. There is a limitation on the extent of distribution of gifts.

Furthermore, it appears from the Scriptures that there is a
limitation in respect to the fact that some gifts were specifically for the beginning of the church. Apostles and prophets
are said to have been given for the founding era of the body
of Christ (Eph 2:20). The first generation of Christians experienced spectacular signs and wonders which the second
generation apparently did not (Heb 2:3-4). Even the gift
of tongues evidently died out before the gift of prophecy
(which was for the founding period of the church) was withdrawn (1 Co 13:8).[2] Nevertheless, any gift even though
given only once is a gift to the whole church, for all benefit
even though remotely from its being given.

The list of gifts. Lists of specific gifts are found in Romans
12:6-8, 1 Corinthians 12:8-10, 28-30 and Ephesians 4:11. Included are apostleship, prophecy, miracles, healing, tongues,

evangelism, pastoring, ministering or helps, teaching, faith, exhortation, discerning spirits, knowledge, showing mercy, giving, administration. Although the list is a full one, it may or may not be complete; but, if not, any other gifts not specified as such in the Bible would have to be similar in their origin and purpose of edifying the body of Christ. Natural talents are probably to be distinguished from spiritual gifts, and they are often, like music, vehicles for the use of spiritual gifts.

The development of spiritual gifts. Although the Spirit is the source of spiritual gifts, the believer may have a part in their development. "But covet earnestly the best gifts" (1 Co 12:31) means that we do have a part to play in being zealous for (covet) better gifts. "Ver. 31a corrects the inference which an indolent nature or weak judgment might draw from vv. 29 f., supposing that God's sovereign ordination supersedes man's effort. Our striving has a part to play, along with God's bestowment, in spiritual acquisitions; hence the contrastive *but*."[3] For instance, the basic gift of helps obviously requires self-discipline for its fullest development.

Too, we can develop our gifts by benefiting from the ministry of others (see Ro 1:11 where Paul is not saying that he could bestow gifts but that he could through his ministry impart the benefit of his spiritual gifts to others). This should be a never ending cycle — gifted people ministering to others who are thereby built up and who in turn minister to others who are then built up to minister to others, etc. This is the way the body of Christ grows quantitatively and qualitatively.

The discovery of one's gifts. But how can one know what his gifts are? Here are three suggestions: First, be informed as to what spiritual gifts are available. A person may not know, for instance, that showing mercy is a spiritual gift; yet this is one everyone could use. Don't limit God—He may want to bring to light and usefulness many gifts in your life before it is over. Second, be willing to do anything for the

Lord. Many Christians miss the full use of their gifts simply because they will not tie themselves down to a regular job in the church. Third, be active, for the use of one gift may lead to the discovery of others. When we are first introduced to Philip in the New Testament he was using the gift of serving (Ac 6:5), and because he was faithful in that, God added the gift of evangelism (Ac 8:5). Faithful use of what we have will bring enlarged opportunities and the gifts to go with them.

HE FILLS

From the perspective of daily living and a vital Christian experience, the filling of the Spirit is undoubtedly the most important aspect of this doctrine. This is the pure essence of true spirituality and the basic requirement for growth and maturity.

What is the filling of the Spirit? The clue for a proper definition of the filling of the Spirit appears in Ephesians 5: 18: "And be not drunk with wine, wherein is excess; but be filled with the Spirit." The comparison between drunkenness and Spirit-filling provides the basic clue: the idea of control. Both drunk and spiritual persons are controlled people, and under the influence of either liquor or the Spirit they do things that are unnatural to them. Looking at the matter another way, we might say that in both cases they lose their self-control and abandon themselves to the influence of either the liquor or the Holy Spirit. This is not to imply that the Spirit-filled life will be erratic or abnormal, but it is to say that it will be a life controlled or governed no longer by self but by the Holy Spirit.

Notice also that the verb "be filled" is a command, not an option. Believers without exception are expected to be filled. This is not something for some select few, but an expected and possible requirement of the normal Christian life.

How often does a person need to be filled? That same verb in Ephesians 5:18, "be filled," answers the question, for it is in the present tense which indicates that the filling is a repeated experience. "Keep on being filled" is a good way to translate it. In other words, a Christian may be filled and filled and filled again. This is illustrated in the experience of the apostles during the early months of the church. On the day of Pentecost they were filled (Ac 2:4). A short time later, after a prayer meeting for boldness, the same group was filled again (Ac 4:31). It is rather important to notice that the apostles did not need to be filled this second time because some specific sin had come into their lives but because they needed control in a new area (boldness to witness) in the face of a new problem (the prohibition to speak by the Sanhedrin). In other words, repeated fillings may be necessary because new areas of life come to light which need to be brought under the control of the Spirit. Of course, it is also true that a Christian needs to be filled again and again when sin (which is ego control) breaks the control of the Spirit.

What are the conditions for being filled? A lot of Christians think that filling comes in answer to some sort of tarrying or agonizing prayer. But we search the New Testament in vain to find an example of believers praying for the filling of the Spirit after the day of Pentecost. The nearest thing to such an example is Paul's prayer for the believers in Ephesus (Eph 1:17), yet even this is not a prayer for filling. Even though tarrying or agonizing in prayer are not required, there are conditions which must be met in order to be Spirit-filled.

First, if the filling involves control, then there must be a dedication of self to God for His use and control. So the first condition is a dedicated life. This involves an initial, crisislike act of dedication in which one gives his life to God for His will to be done through it. Although initial dedication may be brought about by some particular problem, it is not a dedication to do something or to give up something, but a complete settling of the question, Who will run my life?

But there must also be continual dedication and commitment to keep on doing the will of God. When questions arise, the Spirit will guide us to make the right decisions (Ro 8:14), and He does that through our fellowship with Himself which enables Him to tell us what to do. Ideally, a dedicated person at the crossroads of decision does not debate whether or not he will do the will of God but only asks what is the will of God in order that he may do it.

Second, Spirit-filling involves not grieving the Spirit (Eph 4:30). What is it that grieves Him? The answer is sin, but specifically sins of speech, for in the immediate context of that verse the tongue and what it says are mentioned several times.

Third, the Spirit-filled life is a life of dependence (Gal 5: 16). Walking by its very nature is a succession of dependent acts. When one foot is lifted in order to place it in front of the other one, it is done in faith that the foot remaining on the ground will support the full weight of the body. Each foot in turn acts as a support while the other foot is being moved forward. If you can't trust each foot to hold the other in turn then you will stand still. Progress can be made only by trusting. So it is in the Christian life. We make progress as we depend on the Spirit and let Him have full control.

To be Spirit-filled is to be Spirit-controlled, and this means dedication of life, putting away sin, and constant dependence on His power. Prayer and human resolve may often be involved in meeting these conditions; but when they are met, the Spirit's control automatically follows. When the conditions are met, the filling will be experienced.

What are the results of being filled? There are at least four results or characteristics of a Spirit-filled life. The first is Christlikeness, for the fruit of the Spirit (inseparably linked to the filling in Gal 5) is Christlikeness. The second is worship and praise, for the classic verse on filling (Eph 5:18) is followed immediately by a statement of the consequences of being filled — singing and being thankful. The third is submissiveness (Eph 5:21). Spirit control affects all the relationships of life so that proper harmony will be experienced between husbands and wives, parents and children, employers and employees. Self-control will disrupt that harmony.

The fourth result of filling is service for the Lord. What kind of service? The all-inclusive answer is service which in the power of the Spirit uses one's particular combination of spiritual gifts. But, more specifically, Spirit-filling will result in people coming to the Lord in salvation. This was what happened in the book of Acts when people were Spirit-filled. Compare Acts 2:4 with 2:41; 4:8 and 31 with 5:14; 6:3 with 6:7 and 11:24.

Can you ever say that you are filled with the Spirit? If you've ever been in a meeting where the speaker has asked those who are filled to raise their hands, you probably saw much hesitation to do so. Sometimes the speaker will then urge the people to yield themselves and then stand up and declare that they are then filled. Which is right — the reluctance which most seem to have or the aggressiveness that some do have? In a certain sense both emphases are correct. On the one hand it is true that when one yields control to the Spirit, the Spirit does take over and fill that life. On the other hand the hesitation comes from a realization that no one has arrived and there will always be additional areas of life which will need to be brought under the Spirit's control. One can know he is filled and at the same time realize that tomorrow he will need to be filled again.

HE TEACHES

One of the last promises that the Lord made before His crucifixion was that the Holy Spirit would teach the disciples the many things they could not then understand because He had not yet been crucified (Jn 16:12-15). The content of the Spirit's ministry encompasses "all the truth" (the definite article appears in the Greek text) which means revelation about Christ Himself. Peter's clear understanding of Jesus as Lord and Christ on the day of Pentecost is an indication of the Spirit's teaching him this truth (Ac 2:36). Of course our information about Christ now comes from the Bible, so the Spirit must teach the believer the content of Scripture. This will also include information about prophecy ("things to come").

How does the Spirit teach believers? Normally, through using other believers who have and exercise the gift of teaching. This may be through the use of any procedure by which teaching can be done. In other words, the Spirit can use the oral communication of truth or the teaching a man may do through his writings in any era of church history. John's statement in 1 John 2:27 does not mean that human teachers are unnecessary but that his readers needed no one to tell them the truth that he had just declared about antichrists in the group, for the Spirit would confirm that truth to them directly.

HE GUIDES

Romans 8:14 states that one aspect of the Spirit's work is to guide believers, and the book of Acts amply illustrates it (Ac 8:29; 10:19-20; 13:2, 4, 16:6-7; 20:22-23). He will never lead in a manner contrary to the Word of God but always on the basis of it, for the Bible tells us both how God will not lead and how He will lead. The Spirit may then use various means or no means, but ultimately knowing the will of God is walking in such close fellowship with the Lord that you know what the Spirit directs you to do.

HE GIVES ASSURANCE

The Spirit assures us that we are God's children (Ro 8:16). This position also makes us heirs of God with Jesus Christ. Undoubtedly assurance is given to the Christian through an increased understanding of some of the things God does when He saves a person. Thus the Spirit's work of assuring may involve His ministry of teaching. For instance, assurance will deepen when we understand what it means to be sealed with the Spirit and to have the Spirit as an earnest of the completion of our redemption. Understanding what it means to be joined to the risen, undying body of Christ will also nurture assurance.

HE PRAYS

The Spirit is involved in our praying in two ways. First, He guides and directs us as we pray so that we bring to God those petitions which are in His will (Eph 6:19). Second, He prays through us with "groanings which cannot be uttered" (Ro 8:26). The fact of this praying is perfectly clear, though the ramifications of it are not. The verse says that the Spirit helps us, which literally means that He puts His hand to the work of praying in cooperation with us. Apparently the groanings do not find expression, for they are unuttered, but they issue in prayer that is according to the will of God.

THE WORK OF THE SPIRIT IN THE FUTURE

IN THE TRIBULATION PERIOD

Assuming the viewpoint that the church will be raptured before the tribulation begins, this means that His indwelling presence in the temple of God, the church, will be removed (because the temple is), but it does not mean, as is so often assumed, that He will cease to work. We know that multitudes will be saved during the tribulation days (Rev 7:14), and presumably the Spirit will be the Agent of their regeneration. Israelites who successfully come through the judgment at the close of the tribulation period will acknowledge their Redeemer through the ministry of the Spirit (Zec 12:10).

Little is specifically said concerning His work among be-

lievers in this period. If His ministries follow the pattern of
His work in the Old Testament then He will indwell and
empower His people and use them in special service. For
whatever purpose Joel 2 was quoted in Acts 2 it obviously
did not have a complete fulfillment on the day of Pentecost.
The ultimate fulfillment awaits the tribulation days, since
the passage expressly links the pouring out of the Spirit to
the time when the sun will be turned to darkness and the
moon to blood. These events will occur at the close of the
tribulation just before the second coming of Christ (Mt 24:
29-30). Notice, too, Revelation 11:3-4 which links the ministry of the two witnesses during the tribulation to the power
of the Spirit (Zec 4:6).

IN THE MILLENNIAL KINGDOM

The new covenant promises the salvation of Israel during
the kingdom age and the Spirit's indwelling of their lives
(Jer 31:31-34; Eze 36:27). Also during the millennial kingdom the fullness of the Spirit on Christ the King will be evident (Is 11:2-3). That time will involve the fullest display
of the presence and power of God that the earth has ever
known since the days of Adam; and, although little is said
specifically concerning the Spirit's work, His ministry along
with the other Persons of the Trinity will be abundantly displayed.

5

The World of Angels
(including demons and Satan)

THE WORLD OF ANGELS is much more believed in today than it was a generation ago. Churches of Satan receive wide publicity, and respected periodicals occasionally report on demon activities in various places. Consequently the world of people is more aware of the possibility, at least, of the reality of the world of spirits.

THE DOCTRINE OF ANGELS

DO ANGELS REALLY EXIST?

Nobody can prove conclusively that angels do not exist, since no human being can know all the possible creatures that could exist. The best one can do is to say that as far as his human knowledge is concerned he does not *believe* angels could exist. And yet, many do acknowledge, apart from what the Bible says, that there seems to be an order of creatures above human beings. Of course, if one admits the biblical evidence, there is no problem in proving the existence of angels. Indeed, the evidence is overwhelming.

The teaching about angels is widely diffused throughout Scripture. The mention of angels is not confined to one book or one writer or one period. Their existence is mentioned in at least thirty-four books of the Bible and from the earliest (whether Job or Genesis) to the last. Furthermore, our Lord spoke of the real existence of angels on occasions when it would not have been necessary to do so. Some have tried to claim that Christ spoke of angels and demons and Satan simply because He was accommodating Himself to the ignorance of the people of His time. In other words, they claim that He was playing to the grandstands when He talked about spirit beings. But there are instances when this could not have been His motive, so the only conclusion one can reach is that He too believed in their real existence (Mt 18: 10; 26:53).

WHAT ARE ANGELS LIKE?

Angels are personal beings; that is, they possess intelligence (1 Pe 1:12), feelings (Lk 2:13) and will (Jude 6). They are spirit beings (Heb 1:14), though unlike God. They are limited by having some sort of angelic bodies, yet they are not so limited as man is. Apparently they are without the power to reproduce after their kind; that is, baby angels are never born (Mk 12:25); they do not die (Lk 20:36); and they are always designated by the masculine gender in the Scriptures (Gen 18:1-2, but see Zec 5:9 for a possible exception). They have wings with which they fly (Is 6:2), and they are innumerable (Heb 12:22).

But one of the most interesting characteristics of angels is the fact that they are organized. Michael is the only angel designated an archangel (Jude 9) though there may be others (since in Dan 10:13 he is called one of the chief princes). Under these top rulers there seem to be other governmental angel functionaries (Eph 3:10). Believers seem to have a guardian angel assigned to them (Heb 1:14), as do children (Mt 18:10). Some apparently have to do particularly with the worship of God (the seraphim, Is 6:1-3), and others guard His holiness (cherubim, Gen 3:22-24). There is a very important practical point to this: If angels need to be organized in order to do God's will effectively, then so do God's people need to be organized for the same reason.

WHAT DO ANGELS DO?

The ministry of angels seems to fall into well-defined categories involving their work on behalf of various individuals or groups.

Their ministry to Christ. There was an extra measure of angelic activity during our Lord's lifetime. For instance, they predicted His birth (Lk 1:26-33), they announced His birth (Lk 2:13), they protected Him as a baby (Mt 2:13), they strengthened Him after His temptation (Mt 4:11), they were prepared to defend Him from His enemies (though He did not call upon them, Mt 26:53), they strengthened Him in Gethsemane (Lk 22:43), they rolled away the stone from the tomb and announced His resurrection (Mt 28:2, 6).

Their ministry to believers. In general angels help believers (Heb 1:14). Specifically, this may include being involved in answering prayer (Ac 12:7), giving encouragement in times of danger (Ac 27:23-24) and caring for believers at death (Lk 16:22; Jude 9). In addition, believers minister to angels by showing them what redemption means in life (1 Co 4:9; Lk 15:10).

Their ministry to the nations of the world. We have already noticed that Michael is designated the archangel. He is also specially related to Israel as her guardian (Dan 12:1). It seems, too, that other nations have angels assigned to them (Dan 10:21). Clearly, angels will be involved in executing the judgments of the tribulation period on the nations of the world at that time (Rev 8, 9, 16).

Their ministry to unbelievers. It was an angel who smote Herod which resulted in his death as punishment for his arrogance (Ac 12:23). At the end of the age, angels will act as the reapers who separate the righteous from the wicked (Mt 13:39).

These are some of the things good angels do. Evil angels are also involved in the affairs of men and the world, but more of this later. Of course, God would not have to use angels in carrying out the details of His plan, but He has chosen to do so. This does not mean that we worship angels any more than we would worship the circumstances or the friends God might use in carrying out His plan. But since He has chosen to use them, we should give due consideration and thanks to God for angels. In an old church in Scotland are inscribed these words which put the matter in proper balance: "Though God's Power Be Sufithink to Governe Us, Yet for Man's Infirmitie He appointeth His Angels to Watch over Us."

THE DOCTRINE OF SATAN

DOES SATAN REALLY EXIST?

Like the matter of the existence of angels, the existence of Satan probably could not be proved to the man who refuses to accept the evidence of the Bible on the subject. But if he did he would find ample evidence. It is (1) widespread (found in at least seven Old Testament books and referred to by every New Testament writer) and (2) based on Christ's own words (Mt 13:39; Lk 10:18; 11:18). Again these are instances where He did not need to speak of Satan if He were merely accommodating His teaching to the supposed ignorant beliefs of the people.

WHAT IS SATAN LIKE?

Satan is a real personality. The Bible teaches that he possesses intelligence (2 Co 11:3), has emotions (Rev 12:17) and has a will (2 Ti 2:26). Furthermore, he is treated by God as a morally responsible person, not a thing (Mt 25:41).

Satan is a creature, not the Creator (Eze 28:14). Therefore, he does not possess attributes which God alone has, like omnipresence, omniscience and omnipotence. In other words, he possesses creaturely limitations. To be sure, he is of a higher order of creatures than human beings are, but he is not God. Furthermore, because he is a creature, the Creator can and sometimes does place additional limitations on him (Job 1:12).

He is a spirit being. He belonged to the order of angels called cherubim (Eph 6:11-12; Eze 28:14). Apparently he was the highest created angel (Eze 28:12), and because of this retains a great deal of power even in his fallen state (see his being called "the god of this age," 2 Co 4:4, ASV margin, and "the prince of the power of the air," Eph 2:2).

He is an antagonist of God and His people. The very name *Satan* means adversary (see 1 Pe 5:8), while the word *devil* means slanderer (see Rev 12:10). His contentious character is seen also in other designations which the Scripture gives to him, namely, evil one (1 Jn 5:19, ASV), tempter (1 Th 3:5), murderer (Jn 8:44), liar (Jn 8:44), confirmed sinner (1 Jn 3:8). In order to promote this opposition, Satan can appear like a wily serpent (Rev 12:9), or a ferocious dragon (Rev 12:3), or an attractive angel of light (2 Co 11: 14). These abilities obviously make him more deceptive in carrying out his program.

WHAT WAS SATAN'S SIN?

Satan's sin was done from a privileged position. He was not a deprived creature who had not drunk deeply of the blessings of God before he sinned. Indeed, Ezekiel 28:11-15 declares some astounding things about the privileged position in which he sinned. That this passage has Satan in view seems most likely if one eliminates the idea that it is a mythical tale of heathen origin and if one takes the language at all plainly and not merely as filled with Oriental exaggerations. Ezekiel "saw the work and activity of Satan, whom the king of Tyre was emulating in so many ways."[1] Satan's privileges included (1) full measure of wisdom (v. 12), (2) perfection in beauty (v. 12), (3) dazzling appearance (v. 13), (4) a place of special prominence as the anointed cherub that covered God's throne (v. 14). Verse 15 (ASV) says all that the Bible says about the origin of sin — "till unrighteousness was found in thee." It is clear, however, that Satan was not created as an evil being, for the verse clearly declares he was perfect when created. Furthermore, God did not make him sin; he sinned of his own volition and assumed full responsibility for that sin; and because of his great privileges, it is obvious that Satan sinned with full knowledge.

Satan's sin was pride (1 Ti 3:6). The specific details of how that pride erupted are given in Isaiah 14:13-14 and are summarized in the assertion, "I will be like the most High" (v. 14).

HAS SATAN BEEN JUDGED OR WILL HE BE?

Satan has been judged and he will be judged again. There are at least six judgments which Satan has experienced or will experience: (1) He was barred from his original privileged position in heaven (Eze 28:16). (2) A judgment was pronounced on him in the Garden of Eden after the temptation of Adam and Eve (Gen 3:14-15). (3) The central judgment (because it is the basis of all others) was at the cross (Jn 12:31). (4) He will be barred from all access to heaven during the tribulation period (Rev 12:13). (5) At the beginning of the millennium he will be confined in the abyss (not, as incorrectly translated, bottomless pit) (Rev 20:2). (6) At the conclusion of the millennium he will be cast into the lake of fire for all eternity (Rev 20:10)

WHAT DOES SATAN DO?

Satan's avowed purpose is to thwart the plan of God in every area and by every means possible. To accomplish this he is promoting a world system of which he is the head and which stands in opposition to God and His rule in this universe. However, instead of promoting a kingdom whose characteristics are exactly opposite to the features of God's rule, he seeks to counterfeit God's program. Counterfeiting, of course, has a single purpose, and that is to create something as similar to the original as possible and to do it by means of a shortcut.

1. In relation to the redemption of Christ, Satan tried in the temptation to offer Him the rewards of redemption without the suffering of the cross (Mt 4:1-11). (See also Mt 2:

16, Jn 8:44, Mt 16:23 and Jn 13:27 for other attempts to thwart Christ's purpose).

2. In relation to the nations of the world, Satan has been and is deceiving them particularly into thinking they can do what God alone can do (Rev 20:3). At the close of the tribulation period he will gather them together to the Battle of Armageddon (Rev 16:13-14).

3. In relation to unbelievers, Satan blinds their minds so that they will not accept the gospel (2 Co 4:4). He often does this by making them think that any way to heaven is as acceptable as any other. If the Word is planted, then he comes and snatches it away (Lk 8:12).

4. In relation to the believer, Satan may tempt him to lie (Ac 5:3), will accuse and slander him (Rev 12:10), hinders his work for God in any way possible (1 Th 2:18), employs demons to try to defeat him (Eph 6:11-12), tempts him to immorality (1 Co 7:5), sows tares among believers in order to deceive (Mt 13:38-39), and sometimes incites persecutions against them (Rev 2:10). In addition to these specifics he is always trying to get the Christian to follow a counterfeit plan instead of doing the will of God. This will, if possible, involve doing "good" (but not the best), though it may at times involve doing evil.

WHAT IS THE BELIEVER'S DEFENSE AGAINST SATAN?

1. Twice in the New Testament we are told that the Lord lives in heaven to make intercession for His people (Ro 8:34; Heb 7:25). This includes His asking the Father to keep His children from the evil one (Jn 17:15).

2. The believer should also realize that on occasion God may use Satan to teach a particular lesson. When this happens, then the Christian's defense is to learn the lesson God has and to learn it well. This is what occurred with Job and Paul (2 Co 12:7-10).

3. It is also necessary to have the proper attitude toward Satan. Though we have the power of God on our side, it is

never wise to assume that victory is automatically guaranteed. Learn not to speak contemptuously of Satan's power but rather to depend on the Lord for victory (Jude 8-9).

4. The believer should be informed and thereby alert to Satan's attacks (1 Pe 5:8).

5. Taking a decisive stand is also required (Ja 4:7) and then using this stand as a base of operations on which to wage the continual warfare against our enemy.

6. God has provided armor for our defense (Eph 6:11-18). Each piece is important and serves its own special purpose. But we must take the armor which is offered and use it for our protection.

THE DOCTRINE OF DEMONS

WHO ARE THE DEMONS?

The origin of demons has been a matter of speculation for centuries, not only among Christian thinkers but also among the heathen. The Greeks said that they were the souls of departed evil people. Some Christian writers have suggested that demons are the disembodied spirits of a pre-Adamic race. Though there is nothing antiscriptural about this view, there is nothing scriptural about it either, for the Bible nowhere speaks of the existence of such a race. More likely, demons are angels who fell with Satan who is called the prince of the demons (Mt 12:24). However, it is quite clear in the Bible that there are two groups of fallen angels — one that have a certain freedom to oppose God and His people and another who are confined (2 Pe 2:4; Jude 6). Though there is considerable (and often needlessly heated) disagreement over why this second group is in prison, it seems that it is because they are the ones who committed the unnatural sin recorded in Genesis 6:2-4. Even among those demons who are relatively free, the activities of some seem to be restricted to certain periods of history (see Rev 9:14; 16:14). Thus my suggestion concerning the origin of demons looks like this:

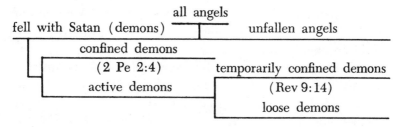

WHAT ARE DEMONS LIKE?

Since demons belong to the same order of being as angels, they possess similar characteristics. They are spirit beings, though this does not mean they are omnipresent. Exactly the opposite is true — they are localized at any given moment. Notice that the demon in Matthew 17:18 is called an unclean spirit in the parallel account in Mark 9:25.

Demons, like angels and Satan, display a great deal of intelligence. The Bible gives indications that they knew Jesus (Mk 1:24), they knew their own eventual doom (Mt 8:29), they are acquainted with the plan of salvation (Ja 2:19), and they have and promote a well-developed system of their own doctrine (1 Ti 4:1-3). Apparently their doctrinal deception will become increasingly active at the close of the church age.

WHAT DO DEMONS DO?

In general, demons, like Satan, attempt to thwart the purpose of God in every way possible (Dan 10:10-14; Rev 16: 13-16). In doing this they extend Satan's activity, and the very number of demons engaged as emissaries of Satan is what makes Satan seem to be omnipresent, though he is not.

In particular, demons can inflict diseases (Mt 9:33; Lk 13: 11, 16), they can possess animals (Mk 5:13) and, as mentioned above, they promote false doctrine (1 Ti 4:1). Sometimes God uses demons in carrying out His plans (1 Sa 16: 14; 2 Co 12:7). This reminds us that even these creatures are under His complete and constant control.

Demons also seem to be concerned with the affairs of nations. Daniel 10:13 speaks of "the prince of the kingdom of Persia" who seems to be a spirit being who resisted the coming of an angel to bring Daniel a message. That prince was himself resisted by Michael the archangel, which means that he must have been a very powerful demon. We have already seen this same suggestion in the evil power behind Babylon and Tyre (Is 14, Eze 28), and the book of Revelation often gives the idea of evil spirit beings deceiving the nations (Rev 16:13-14). In Isaiah 24:21 (ASV) God finally punishes the "host of the high ones on high, and the kings of the earth upon the earth." A fair conclusion from these passages is simply that there is a cosmic warfare involving the nations of the earth, and some demons are powerful enough to sway the affairs of nations. What this may mean in international affairs is not easy to discern, but that it means something significant even today seems clear.

IS THERE SUCH A THING AS DEMON POSSESSION?

The possibility of demon possession demands serious consideration because not only has it been and is it being accepted as a fact in many places, but apparently the Lord recognized it as a real thing.[2] Furthermore, He and His disciples distinguished between normal physical illnesses which were cured by laying on of hands or anointing with oil, and cases of demon possession which were cured by commanding the demon to come out (Mt 10:8; Mk 6:13).

The only way to try to define demon possession is by the characteristics of the clearly diagnosed cases in the Bible, and this is not easy because sometimes demon possession showed the symptoms of ordinary diseases (Mt 9:32-33). Nevertheless, demon possession seems to mean that a demon or demons reside within a person, exerting direct control on that person's mind and/or body.

It is probably a good idea to make a distinction between demon possession and demon activity or influence, though it may be little more than an academic distinction. If there is a distinction, then in demon possession the base of the demon's operations is within the person possessed, while demon influence is from outside the person's being. However, the symptoms or characteristics may very well be the same whether the demon is operating from within or without. Yet if you ask whether a Christian can be demon possessed, seemingly the answer should be no, simply because the indwelling of the Holy Spirit would seem to forbid a rival power like a demon from also possessing him at the same time. But if you ask whether a Christian can be affected seriously by a demon, the answer is certainly yes; the effect of such demon activity may be the same as characterizes demon possession. As stated, sometimes physical disease is the result of demon possession or activity (Mt 9:32-33), and sometimes mental derangement is due to demons (Mt 17:15), but not always (see Dan 4).

When a person appears with an emotional or mental problem, the cause may be single or multiple, usually the latter, and that is why it is often difficult to unravel the problem. Medical help may be all that is necessary, or it may be required in order to bring the person to the place where a spiritual or demonic problem may then be dealt with. Demons can be cast out, but this is no light thing. The Lord reminded us that there is the danger of a demon returning to his former victim accompanied by worse spirits (Lk 11:24-26). Also, when a demon is cast out he will undoubtedly seek embodiment in some other person.[3]

THE DESTINY OF DEMONS

Some demons are temporarily confined. For instance, some who were free during the lifetime of Christ were cast into the abyss (Lk 8:31), and some who are now confined will be loosed to do their work during the coming tribulation days (Rev 9:1-11; 16:13-14). However, eventually all demons will be cast with Satan into the lake of fire forever (Mt 25:41).

6

The Nature of Man

THE QUESTION, What is man? is without doubt the most basic of philosophical, theological and practical questions. Man is only a body, says the materialist. Man's body is nothing but an idea, says the idealist. Actually, says the pragmatist, we know nothing of either material or immaterial entities — only relationships. Bound up with these viewpoints are answers to the all-important questions, Where did we come from? Why are we here? Where are we going? Philosophy has concerned itself with the study of these questions, and the various philosophies of the ages have made numerous attempts to give answers. The very number of such philosophical schemes and the variety of their answers show how really uncertain men are about these important answers. While philosophy may teach us what men have thought about man, only the Bible can give an authoritative and complete picture of the nature of man, and correct answers to the basic questions concerning him.

THE CHARACTER OF MAN

MAN IS A CREATED BEING

One's view of the origin of man will affect his entire understanding of and attitude toward man. If, for instance, man is the product of evolution, then the extent of the effects of sin and the need of a Saviour are played down, if not eliminated. If, on the other hand, man was created by God, then this concept carries with it the companion idea of the responsibility of man. If God created man, then there is Someone outside of man to whom he becomes responsible.

He is not in and of himself the master of his own fate or completely at the mercy of fate; he is neither the final authority nor the only one to whom he must ultimately answer. A doctrine of creation implies creatures who are responsible to that Creator. The evolutionary origin of man relieves man of responsibility to a personal Creator outside of himself.

Since evolution is so widely taught today at almost every level of education, a few comments about the theory are in order. The theory teaches that all living creatures have developed through natural processes from that first living cell, and there is no clear idea where that cell came from. No Christian denies that there is observable change *within* certain fixed limits (this is evolution in the basic sense of change), but the theory of evolution proposes much more than this — development of new forms, species, and genes.

How did this supposedly happen? It is very important to remember that, according to the evolutionist, the only explanation for all this happening is through mutations accumulating over long periods of time and the good ones being preserved by natural selection so as to form new subspecies, species and families. In other words, the formula is this: mutations + natural selection + time = evolution. Cannon cogently observes, "A fact that has been obvious for many years is that Mendelian mutations deal only with changes in existing characters, never with the appearance of a new functioning character. . . . No experiment has produced progeny that show entirely new functioning organs. And yet it is the appearance of new characters in organisms which marks the boundaries of the major steps in the evolutionary scales."[1] This is a basic and unsolved problem for evolutionists. He has to *believe* that somehow these new things were evolved. For example, a famed anthropologist wrote concerning the development of the vertebrates from the invertebrates: "All this is complicated, obscure, and dubious. Anyway there evolved from the invertebrates a tribe

of animals which, by hook or by crook, acquired back-
bones."[2] That's faith, and not well placed at that!

The fossil record is the record of what supposedly *did
happen;* and if evolution is correct, it should show a gradual
transition from the simplest to the most complex without
systematic or regular gaps. And yet there is among the bil-
lions of known fossils a systematic absence of transitional
forms between all higher categories of life! " 'Links' are missing just where we most fervently desire them and it is all too
probable that many 'links' will continue to be missing."[3]

While there is a variety of opinion over some of the details of what the Bible says about the creation of man, many
of the facts of this matter stand out clearly in the biblical
record. The following are some of them:

1. At least seventeen times in Genesis 1 God is said to be
the Creator. The important thing to consider, however, is,
What God? The answer is: the God whom the writer of
this chapter knew, that is, Moses' God, and Moses knew Him
as a personal, living, miracle-working God. Even if one holds
to the documentary hypothesis, the God of this section
would be the God whom the supposed writer or editor knew,
and this would rule out the idea of His being an impersonal
something. Neither Moses nor a later editor would have had
any difficulty believing in special creation, knowing from experience what he did of God.

2. The Genesis account also tells us something of how God
created. The verb used in Genesis 1:1, 21, and 27 indicates a
great, new, and epoch-making creation. In Genesis 1:1 *creation ex nihilo* is taught, since no preexisting material is mentioned or implied. Other verbs in the chapter say that God
"made," "called," "set," "formed," "caused," "took,"
"planted," etc. In addition, the order of creation "day" by
"day" is indicated from start (1:1) to finish (2:1).

3. Some evidence concerning the time of creation is also
presented in Genesis. A sequence of days begins at 1:3.
There are four views as to the meaning of the days. First,

they are understood to be the days during which God *revealed* the creation scene to Moses. They are "revelatory days" and have nothing to do with the time of creation. Second, they are considered to be ages (for the word *day* is used of a long period of time in the Old Testament, Joel 2: 31). The geologic ages can easily be placed into these age-days. Third, they are seen as literal solar days (now measured by 24 hours) with huge time gaps between them so as to allow for the apparently long ages of geology. Fourth, they are solar days that followed one another in succession and without gaps. This view is supported by the presence of the phrase "evening and morning" with each day, and by the fact that in other places in the Old Testament when a numerical adjective appears with the word *day,* a solar day is meant. By this view the earth as we know it is quite recent, and by the other views of the meaning of day the creation of man is relatively recent in comparison to other aspects of creation.

The relation of Genesis 1:1 to the rest of the chapter is also debated. Some consider it to be a topic sentence, and others understand it to be a statement of an original perfect creation which was ruined for some reason and which ruined condition is described in verse 2. That catastrophe is often said to have been caused by the fall of Satan, but that is not necessary to understanding the passage that way. The cause of the ruin may be unexplained.

4. Undoubtedly the effects of the flood on the world that we know today would have to be a part of anyone's picture of the creation of the world and its condition before the flood. Of course, if the flood was only a local event, then it would have made little difference except locally. But if it was universal and if the waters covered the earth, then that presents ramifications which are staggering to the imagination. Such a flood would easily account for the fossil remains being laid down and would mean that the geologic record does not incorporate long ages of time but was accom-

plished in about a year's time. Arguments for a universal flood are difficult to answer. Note Genesis 7:19-20, the large size of the ark (Gen 6:15 — in fact the ark would seem unnecessary in a local flood), and the use made of the flood in 2 Peter 3:3-7.[4]

5. The origin of the world by the creative acts of God would most likely have included creating some things with the appearance of age. The Genesis account of Adam and Eve's creation indicates that they were at the time of their creation mature people who only appeared to have passed through the normal time-consuming processes of growth but who in reality had not. Some of the trees in the Garden of Eden were likely full grown with the appearance of age. We do know, for instance, that the wine Christ created at Cana (Jn 2) tasted old but actually was not. The same is true for the food that fed the 4,000 people and also the 5,000 — it was only minutes old when distributed, though when eaten it seemed to have passed through the normal processes of maturing. How much of this God did in the various facets of creation we do not know; but that He did it in some instances seems clear.

6. Creation is regarded as an historical fact in many other places in Scripture. Notice Exodus 20:11; 1 Chronicles 1:1; Psalm 8:3-6; Matthew 19:4-5; Mark 10:6-7; Luke 3:38; Romans 5:12-21; 1 Corinthians 11:9; 15:22, 45; 2 Corinthians 11:3; 1 Timothy 2:13-14 and Jude 14. The point is simply this: Even if for some reason one could try to do away with the reliability or historicity of Genesis 1-11, he would not have gotten rid of the biblical teaching on creation (and particularly the historicity of Adam). It is very popular to say that Genesis 1-11 is an allegory, but if it is, then how can these other passages be explained?

MAN IS A MULTIFACETED BEING

Basically man is material (body) and immaterial (soul or spirit). Both aspects were the direct result of God's creative activity (Gen 2:7) in which He made man in His image and likeness (Gen 1:26; 5:1). It is this resemblance to God that makes man uniquely significant, and whatever happened in the fall of man into sin did not completely erase that image (notice 1 Co 11:7 and Ja 3:9, where exhortations are based on the fact that man possesses the image of God). What is that image?

Answers to that question through the years have included that the image is man's physical body, or his capacity for moral and spiritual activity, which ability he still retains, or abilities which are now totally lost. Actually, the truth seems to be a combination of things: the image of God involves man's being given dominion over the earth and his capacity for moral action, both of which have been disturbed by the entrance of sin so that he lost his dominion and corrupted his moral abilities. Nevertheless, he is unique among all God's creatures because of being created in His image.

It is quite obvious that the body of man (his material part) has many functions. Seeing is not the same as hearing. The nervous system is different, separate, and yet related to both seeing and hearing, and so on.

It is probably best to view the immaterial part of man in the same manner. Soul, spirit, heart, mind, will and conscience are all facets of man's immaterial nature, and it is often difficult to make hard and fast distinctions between them. It seems to be an oversimplification to say that man is body, soul and spirit, for soul and spirit do not fully categorize the immaterial part of man, and they are not always distinct. For instance, we are told to love God with the soul (Mt 22:37), and the flesh wars against the soul (1 Pe 2:11). The spirit can magnify the Lord (Lk 1:46-47), and yet it can partake of corruption (2 Co 7:1). In some instances it appears that the spirit is related to higher aspects of man's nature (and all men, including the unsaved, have a spirit, 1 Co 2:11).

The "heart" (not the organ, of course) seems to be the

most inclusive concept of all aspects of the immaterial part of
man. It is said to be the seat of man's intellectual life (Mt
15:19-20), his emotional life (Ps 37:4; Ro 9:2), his volitional
life (Ex 7:23; Heb 4:7), and his spiritual life (Ro 10:9-10;
Eph 3:17).

Conscience is a witness within man which has been affected by the fall of man but which still can be a guide for
both the unbeliever and the believer. Notice Romans 2:15
and 1 Timothy 4:2 in relation to the unbeliever. As far as
the believer is concerned, his conscience may lead him in
right relationships to his government (Ro 13:5), his employer
(1 Pe 2:19), and his brethren (1 Co 8:7, 10, 12).

The mind of the unsaved man is given some very uncom-
plimentary adjectives in the New Testament. It is reprobate
(Ro 1:28), vain (that is, inappropriate, Eph 4:17), defiled
(Titus 1:15), darkened (Eph 4:18), and blinded by Satan
(2 Co 4:4). And yet when one accepts Christ as Saviour and
then gives his life to the Lord, an aspect of that dedication
involves the renewing of the mind (Ro 12:2). Then we can
love God (Mt 22:37), understand the Lord's will (Eph 5:
17), and praise Him intelligently (1 Co 14:15).

The will of man is another very important facet of our immaterial natures. The will of an unsaved man may effect a
good action (Ac 27:43), as can the will of a believer (Titus
3:8), but the opposite is also true (1 Ti 6:9; Ja 4:4).

All this discussion points up the fact that the Christian apparently has within himself two different capacities or natures. Before he was saved he had only the capacity to serve
and please self. This old nature or sin nature must be defined not simply in terms of the ability to do evil, because it
is more than that. There are many things which are not evil
in themselves but which originate from the old nature. The
all-inclusive characteristic is that the old nature does that
which leaves God out. At conversion we were given a new
nature or a new capacity with which we may serve God
(study Ro 6:18-20; 2 Pe 1:4; Eph 4:22-25).

However, these two natures or capacities are not like two reels of tape on which are stored separate sets of actions which can be printed out on a computer. In reality, the same action might be initiated by either nature. What distinguishes the old from the new is not necessarily the action itself but the use of it. Thus both reels of tape may have a number of actions on them which are exactly the same (though some things which are clearly evil would only be related to the old nature), and the believer through the action of his will pushes the button which determines which nature is permitted to act.

THE FALL OF MAN

The entire question of why sin was included in the plan of God is ultimately something man cannot answer. But the means by which sin entered the experience of man is clearly detailed in the Bible in Genesis 3. This chapter has its many critics whose views (whether they call it myth, true myth, legend, sacred legend, or whatever) boil down to the fact that they do not consider its contents to be historical. Yet they often try to preserve the "true" character of the non-historical (and thus ultimately false) story. Here is an example of such fancy theological dodging:

> Unless we are invincible fundamentalists we know that Genesis 3 is properly to be regarded a "true myth" — that, though Eden is on no map and Adam's fall fits no historical calendar, that chapter witnesses to a dimension of human experience as present now as at the dawn of history — in plain terms, we are fallen creatures, and the story of Adam and Eve is the story of you and me.[5]

Nevertheless, the structure, details and subsequent references to the story all point to its being historically true (notice especially Mt 19:3-6 and Ro 5:12-21; in addition, Lk 3:38 and Jude 14 show that Adam does not simply mean mankind but an individual person).

THE TEST

The test to which Adam and Eve were put was both extremely significant and relatively minor. It was minor from the viewpoint that a single prohibition in the midst of all the bountiful provision of the Garden of Eden was a relatively minor matter. Not to allow them to know evil experimentally was a blessing from God, not a lack in their lives. Of course, from the other viewpoint, the prohibition was literally a life-or-death matter and of the utmost importance. To keep or break this commandment was the principal means of showing obedience or disobedience to the will of God. (Of course, Adam and Eve did have other responsibilities, like cultivating the garden). Evidently the tree of the knowledge of good and evil was an actual tree which God arranged to be the instrument of conveying that knowledge.

THE COURSE OF THE TEMPTATION

The attack by Satan started with the lure of Genesis 3:1. Satan was evidently trying to get Eve to believe that God was not good if He withheld anything from them. Her reply in verse 2 seems to indicate that she felt that for all practical purposes God had given them everything and the single restriction was really trivial. Satan was trying to sully the goodness of God.[6] "If God were good," Satan was saying, "He would not withhold anything from you. But since He has held back the fruit of this single tree, He cannot be good. By contrast, my plan allows you to do the very thing God will not permit." This was Satan's counterfeit.

The logic behind this approach was in the form of a syllogism. The major premise was: Restrictions are not good. The minor premise was: God's plan is restrictive. The conclusion was: God's plan is not good. In contrast, Satan's unrestricted plan was supposed to be good.

Eve then took a step on her own and rationalized the wrong she was about to do. Examining the forbidden fruit, she reasoned that since it was good for food and since God had committed to her the particular responsibility of preparing an attractive and varied diet for her husband, it could not be too wrong to take that fruit. The same line of argument applied to the beauty of the fruit and its provision of knowledge. Gone from her mind was the central fact that God had expressly forbidden the eating of that particular fruit. Her mind was filled only with the rationalization and, having thus prejustified her action, she and Adam ate in flagrant disobedience to the revealed will of God.

THE RESULTS OF THE SIN

As a result of the sin, the following things occurred:

1. The serpent was condemned to crawl (3:14).

2. Satan was set at enmity with the seed of the woman and permitted to give Christ a painful but not deadly wound (v. 15). However, Satan was condemned to a deadly wound ("head" in contrast to "heel").

3. Eve and women were assigned pain in childbirth and submission to their husbands (v. 16).

4. Adam and men were assigned to unpleasant labor because of the cursing of the ground (vv. 17-19).

5. The race, of course, experienced broken fellowship with God or spiritual death, physical death, and exclusion from the benefits of Eden. Adam and Eve's sin changed the course of history and the lives of all their descendants (read again Ro 5:12-21).

The Sin of Man

A DEFINITION OF SIN

Many definitions of sin have been proposed throughout history, and they divide into fairly well-defined categories.

1. Some say sin is an illusion — it doesn't really exist. To be sure, there are lacks in man, but given time and the ongoing processes of evolution, these will disappear. A medical doctor not long ago said, "There is no place for the concept of

sin in psychotherapy." And very long ago, more than one thinker said that man is conscious of sin only because of his lack of knowledge. If he knew more, he could dissipate that illusion of sin.

2. Sin is an eternal principle of evil outside of God and independent of Him. This is dualism which has been associated in one form or another with Zoroaster, Yang and Yin in Chinese thought, and early Gnosticism.

3. Sin is selfishness. This is a common definition of sin and is scriptural though inadequate, for it is not inclusive enough. For instance, by this definition a man who steals food from the rich to feed the poor may not be acting selfishly, but he nevertheless is sinning. However, much sin is selfishness.

4. The biblical definition of sin in 1 John 3:4 is that it is lawlessness. This simple definition actually needs further explanation, for in order to know what sin is we must define *law*. A definition of *law* will depend on the period of history you are talking about. Law in the Garden of Eden was one thing; law in the time of Abraham, another; in the time of Moses, still another; today, it is the many commands of the New Testament. Thus sin is any deviation from those commands. A summary statement is found in 1 Corinthians 10:31, where believers are told to do everything to the glory of God. So an inclusive definition of *sin* would be anything that does not conform to the glory of God. And, indeed, that is the standard against which sin is measured in the familiar verse, Romans 3:23.

PERSONAL SIN

At least eight basic words for sin are in the Old Testament and at least twelve in the New. They indicate that: (1) there was always a clearly understood standard against which the sin was committed; (2) evil may take a variety of forms; (3) man's responsibility was definite and clearly defined; (4) sin is a positive rebellion against God. Some instructive Scripture verses are: Genesis 38:7; Ezekiel 48:11; 1

Kings 8:50; Matthew 5:21; 1 Corinthians 6:9; Galatians 6:1; 1 Timothy 4:2. Personal sin is not simply missing the mark; for whenever one misses, he hits something. Good omitted means wrong committed.

THE INHERITED SIN NATURE

"By nature" we are children of wrath, declared the apostle (Eph 2:3). This sin nature, which all people have by birth, is that capacity to do those things (good, neutral or bad) which do not commend us to God. The Scriptures are filled with statements of the corruption of many aspects of man's nature. His intellect (2 Co 4:4; Ro 1:28), his conscience (1 Ti 4:2), his will (Ro 1:28), his heart (Eph 4:18), and his total being (Ro 1:18-3:20) have been corrupted. This is the doctrine of total depravity. Total depravity does not mean that everyone is as thoroughly depraved in his actions as he could possibly be, nor that everyone will indulge in every form of sin, nor that a person cannot appreciate and even do acts of goodness; but it does mean that the corruption of sin extends to all men and to all parts of all men so that there is nothing within the natural man that can give him merit in God's sight.

THE IMPUTATION OF SIN

Theologians have long argued over the concept of imputed sin. Many understand it to mean that Adam's first sin was charged to the account of every man that has been born into the world. Others feel that Adam acted as the representative of mankind but without any guilt actually being transferred to others. The debate centers around the meaning of Romans 5:12 and especially the last words in that verse — "all sinned." Do they mean that all are sinners (which is essentially saying that all have a sin nature) or do they mean that in some way all mankind sinned when Adam sinned? If the latter, then this is imputed sin.

Many charge that such a concept of sin could not be correct because it seems not to be fair to be charged with something when you were not even born. Whether this be a logical conclusion or not, it is true that imputation is a recognized idea both in and outside the Scriptures. For an example of imputation in the Bible, read Hebrews 7:9-10. Notice also 1 Samuel 22:15 and 2 Corinthians 5:21 (an undeserved imputation no Christian objects to!). Procedures in courts of law often involve the principle of imputation in this modern day, so the concept is not exceptional at all.

If the concept of imputed sin is a biblical one (and it appears to be), then this along with man's personal sinning and his depraved nature are three reasons why God must condemn all men for their sin.

SIN IN RELATION TO THE CHRISTIAN

The fact of sin. Becoming a Christian does not free one from sinning. Of course there are some who teach eradication of the sin nature in this life, but the pictures and doctrines of the New Testament seem to teach otherwise. In fact, John mentions three false claims which people in his day made in this regard in 1 John 1:8-10. Verse 8 speaks of denying the presence of the principle of sin; verse 9, the denial of particular sins; and verse 10, the denial of personally sinning.

The requirement for the believer. The requirement for the believer is "to walk in the light" (1 Jn 1:7). Fellowship is gained by letting the light reveal right and wrong and then by responding to that light continually. The Christian never becomes light as long as he is in his earthly body, but he can and must walk in response to the light while here on earth. As he does, two things follow: first, fellowship with other believers, and second, cleansing. This cleansing is a result of walking in the light, not of confession of sins committed. In other words, walking in the light shows up our sins and frailties; thus we need constant cleansing, and this is available on the basis of the death of Christ. Walking in the light illumines areas of darkness which are immediately confessed; walking in that increased light illumines further areas of darkness, and so on and on throughout the Christian life. This is a requirement that is tailored automatically to every believer's spiritual need at any given moment in his spiritual pilgrimage.

The preventives for sin. It is always better to be vaccinated than to have the illness, and God has provided some preventives for sin in the believer's life. One is the Word of God (Ps 119:11). Another is the constant intercession of Christ (Jn 17:15), and a third is the work of the Holy Spirit in the believer's life, doing such things as producing effective Christian service (Jn 7:37-39).

The penalties for sin. (1) Any sin brings a certain loss of fellowship between the believer and his heavenly Father (1 Jn 1:6). (2) Certain sins may require the local church to take action excommunicating the erring brother, but always with the hope and always working toward his ultimate restoration (1 Co 5:4-5). (3) Chastisement which may take many forms is also sometimes a penalty for persistent sin (Heb 12:6). (4) On occasion the Lord may take a believer to heaven through physical death because of his habitual sinning (1 Co 11:30).

The remedy for sin. Whenever it comes to our attention that we have sinned, then we should readily and willingly acknowledge it. The word *confess* means, literally, to say the same thing; that is, to agree or to acknowledge fully (1 Jn 1:9). When a believer confesses his sin, he agrees with what God says about that sin and acknowledges his past disagreement or guilt. Confession is not mere mouthing of something so as to automatically grind out forgiveness. There must be an element of repentance and a desire to forsake that sin (Ac 19:18). And yet, who hasn't fallen back into the same sin that he has confessed, often over and over again? This does not necessarily indicate that something was deficient about the confession. It may only mean that the means for victory were not appropriated.

Since it is fellowship within the family of God that is broken by sin, then it is that same fellowship that is restored when confession is made. Sin does not expel one from the family, but it does hinder full enjoyment of the family life. Confession restores that relationship. The eternal fellowship of belonging to the family can never be broken, but fellowship within the family can be interrupted by sin. Sin may also affect other members of the family, so that appropriate steps may have to be taken to restore those relationships as well. Sin is always a serious matter, for it affects God, others and ourselves.

7

Christ's Salvation

THE DOCTRINE OF SALVATION is both simple and complex. On the one hand, most can quote at least a part of John 3:16 or Paul's response to the Philippian jailor's question about how to be saved. (Ac 16:31). On the other hand, who can explain how a holy God-man could become sin and die, or who can fathom the concept of election (so much a part of the doctrine of salvation)? Salvation is an extremely important doctrine to understand correctly, for an anathema (curse) is placed on anyone (including angels, or any preacher) who presumes to proclaim a different gospel from the true one. Thus it is rather important to understand and be able to explain the gospel of salvation accurately and clearly. How little this is done is all too evident from many tracts one picks up or sermons heard on the radio which confuse the gospel.

Of course, the doctrine of salvation is inseparably connected with the doctrine of Christ already studied in this book. The reason for this vital link is obvious: The worth of salvation depends on the worth of the Saviour. If He were sinful like every other man, then His death could pay for no more than His own sins. Just as the Passover lamb had to be proved to be without blemish before it was slain (Ex 12:5-6), so the life of our Lord proved Him to be the perfect and sinless sacrifice for our sins. However, since we have already considered these matters in chapter 4 we shall concentrate here on His work of redemption, including the many facets of that salvation.

WHAT IS INVOLVED IN ELECTION?

There is no debate about the fact that election is a difficult doctrine by anybody's standard, but since it is a scriptural doctrine we cannot dodge it. And, of course, it is a doctrine that is inseparably connected with the doctrine of salvation.

THE CONCEPT

The principle of election is around us everywhere, admittedly not the concept of election unto salvation, but the principle of selection which is just a softer word for election. We were born into different families; our IQ's are not the same; we are of different races; we have varied opportunities in life, etc. All of these things which we take for granted involve the selectivity of chance, fate, circumstances or something.

The Bible doctrine of election also involves this principle of differentiation. It may be defined as the action of God in choosing certain people for certain purposes. The reason the definition is so broad is so that it can include the various people and groups who are said to be elect in the Bible. For example, (1) Israel as a nation was elect (Deu 4:37; 1 Ch 16:13). The group included both regenerated and unregenerated people. (2) King Cyrus is also called God's chosen one, though he was an unsaved man as far as we know (Is 45:1-4). (3) Christ is said to be God's elect (Is 42:1). (4) There will be an elect people during the tribulation days who are differentiated from the church (Mt 24:22, 24, 31). (5) Today there is an election of God — those who are believers in Christ (Col 3:12; Titus 1:1). In relation to this last group, election may be defined as the action of God in choosing those who will be saved as members of the body of Christ.

The concept of election must be rooted in the character of God Himself. In other words, election, as everything God does, is in complete harmony with His character. This means several things:

1. Election is loving, for God who is love can do nothing unloving (Eph 1:4 — the words "in love" may just as well be the opening words of v. 5 as the closing words of v. 4).

2. God's election is wise because He is wise (Jude 25).

3. His elective purpose originated in eternity past (Eph 1: 4) and extends throughout eternity future (Ro 8:30).

4. The outworking of election will not generally violate natural laws which God created and to which He normally binds Himself. This means that the elect will not be saved through an angel suddenly appearing and preaching to them, but through the normal process of hearing and believing the witness that comes from other human beings (Ro 10:14). It also means that the natural law of sowing and reaping applies, so an unbeliever who persists in his unbelief will reap the lake of fire. In other words, the element of the exercise of human responsibility is part of the total program of election.

5. Election ultimately glorifies God (Eph 1:12-14). In some instances this is difficult for us to see. But we must remember that we observe only a very small part of the outworking of God's total program in this universe, and we really are in no position to pass judgment on what He is doing.

THE SCRIPTURAL BASIS

The principal passages that speak of election in the New Testament are Ephesians 1:3-14, Romans 9:6-24, 8:28-30, John 6:44, Acts 13:48, 1 Peter 2:8, and Revelation 17:8. These passages deal with the questions of our rights versus God's right to elect, the pretemporal choice of those whom He would save, and the passing by of others. Many things in these passages are not easy, but if we can begin to believe them (even though we do not fully understand), then we are beginning to see election from God's viewpoint.

THE OUTWORKING

Clearly there is a people *who have been chosen.* Ephesians 1:4-5 show that this group was chosen in love before the foundation of the world. Verses like 2 John 1, 13, Romans

16:13, and Galatians 1:15-16 show that this group is composed of elect individuals, and verses like John 13:18, Romans 9:22, and 1 Peter 2:8 indicate that some were not included in the group. We do not know the answer to the question of what prompted God to choose as He did, but we do know that He never acts contrary to His character. Election is more than just foreseeing who would eventually believe; it is action of choosing those who would believe.

There is a procedure *which brings to fruition that pretemporal act of electing.* That procedure includes sending the Saviour to die, all the necessary acts of the period of His incarnation, the preaching of the gospel today, and the requirement of faith in order to be saved. Election does not obliterate human responsibility. Men everywhere are commanded to believe (Ac 16:31; 17:30), and no one is saved without believing (Eph 2:8-9). Let us put it this way: there are unsaved elect people alive today, who, though elect, are now lost and will not be saved until they believe. Even if this seems paradoxical, it is true, and not to recognize it is not to see all aspects of this doctrine.

There is a product *of election and that is a people who do good works (Eph 2:10).* It is in our identity as the "elect of God" that we are to put on "mercies, kindness, humbleness of mind, meekness, longsuffering" (Col 3:12). Trying to comprehend the sovereignty of God should never lead to license but to an amazement that humbles and a gratitude that sanctifies (Ro 11:33-36).

The Death of Christ

ITS ACCOMPLISHMENTS

It was a substitution for sin. There are many facets to the meaning of Christ's death, but the central one — without which the others have no eternal meaning — is substitution. This simply means that Christ died in the place of sinners. The use of the Greek preposition *anti* clearly teaches this because it means "in the place of." It is used, for instance, with this meaning in a passage that has nothing to do with the death of Christ (Lk 11:11). But more significantly, it is used in a passage which gives our Lord's own interpretation of the meaning of His death (Mt 20:28; Mk 10:45). His death, He said, was to be a payment in the place of many.

However, another preposition, *huper*, is also used in the New Testament, and it has two meanings: sometimes it means "for the benefit of" and sometimes "in the place of." Of course the death of Christ was *both* in our place and for our benefit, and there is no reason why *huper* when it is used in relation to His death does not include both ideas. See, for instance, 2 Corinthians 5:21 and 1 Peter 3:18.

There is no debate over the "benefit" meaning of this preposition; the question is whether or not the word also means substitution. If we could find a passage in the New Testament that does not relate to the atonement where the word *huper* means substitution, then we would have good grounds for asserting that it can also mean substitution in atonement passages like those just mentioned. And there is such a passage — Philemon 13.

The picture is clear — Paul in Rome was sending the newly converted slave Onesimus back to the master from whom he had run away, Philemon who lived in Colosse. "Now," said Paul to Philemon, "I would like to have kept Onesimus with me in Rome that in your place [*huper*] he might have ministered unto me in the bonds of the gospel." Its principal meaning cannot be "for Philemon's benefit," for it would have been Paul, not Philemon who would have benefited from Onesimus' staying in Rome and serving Paul in Philemon's place. The point is that if the word can include the idea of substitution in a passage that does not relate to the atonement, it certainly can in those that do. It is also true that the word means substitution outside the New Testament, which further strengthens the argument.[1]

What do those who refuse to admit that the New Testament teaches a doctrine of substitutionary atonement do with

this evidence? Either they submerge substitution in a
whole smorgasbord of other (and usually biblical) benefits
of Christ's death so that it loses its distinctive as the basis of
all other benefits (and without substitution, remember that
there would be no eternal benefits); or they say that the
idea of substitution must be reinterpreted or viewed totally
in the light of benefit only. As an example of the first
"dodge," one writer sets up the smorgasbord by saying, "The
death of Jesus is bigger than any definition, deeper and more
profound than any rationale. . . .By a rich variety of terms
and analogies it is set forth, but it is never completely cap-
tured in any verbal net. . . .Even though no final rationale of
the cross is to be achieved, we must seek its meaning again
and again."[2]

Then the author proceeds to list the following headings in
this order under the general title, "The Meaning of the Death
of Jesus": (1) Christ's death as judgment; (2) Christ's
death as triumph; (3) Liberation at immeasurable cost; (4)
Christ's death as expiation; (5) Christ's death as reconciliation; (6) Christ's death as revelation; (7) Christ's death as
sacrifice; (8) Christ's death as substitution; (9) Existential:
a way of life shared. Not only is substitution decentralized,
but it is also redefined by this author. No reference is made
to the *anti* verses, and substitution is conceived of as Jesus
doing something *in* us and for our benefit, not as our replace-
ment.[3]

Here is an example of the second "dodge" — reinterpreting
substitution in the light of benefit.

> One remark may be made with regard to the theme of
> substitutionary atonement as found in Paul. The fact is
> that he intends what we may call a "representative" rather
> than a "substitutionary" view of Christ's death. When Paul
> writes that Christ died "for" me, he usually means not
> "instead of me" but "for my benefit." . . . Thus it cannot
> be a matter of substitution or of a scapegoat. In another
> context, it is true, the analogy of the ransom of a captive
> or (very rarely) that of a sacrificial offering is brought into

play by Paul and suggests substitution. But this motif . . .
is dominated by the ruling conception of our participa-
tion with Christ in his death to sin and the law.[4]

None of the atonement verses we discussed are even mentioned by this writer. That is hardly indicative of supposedly
unprejudiced liberal scholarship!

It provided redemption from sin. The doctrine of redemption is built on three words in the New Testament. The
first is a simple word which means "to buy or purchase or
pay a price for something." It is used, for instance, with
this ordinary, everyday meaning in the parable of the trea-
sure hid in a field which motivated the man to buy (redeem)
the field (Mt 13:44). In relation to our salvation, the word
means to pay the price which our sin demanded so that we
could be redeemed. Read 2 Peter 2:1, where the extent of
redemption includes paying the price for unsaved false
teachers; Revelation 5:9, where the means is said to be the
blood of Christ; and 1 Corinthians 6:19-20, where the desired
result of redemption is that we might glorify God in our bodies.

The second word is the same basic word indicated above,
prefixed with a preposition which has the force of intensify-
ing the meaning. This can be easily expressed in English because the preposition means "out of," thus making the second
word mean "to purchase out of the market." Thus the idea in
this second word is that Christ's death not only paid the
price for sin but also removed us from the marketplace of sin
in order to give us full assurance that we will never be returned to the bondage and penalties of sin. The purpose of
Christ's death was "to redeem them that were under the law,
that we might receive the adoption of sons" (Gal 4:5). The
compound word is used in this verse and assures us that we
can never lose that adoption as sons and be returned to bondage.

The third word for redemption is an entirely different one.
Its basic meaning is to loose and thus it signifies that the

purchased person is also released and set free in the fullest
sense. The means of this release is through the substitution
Christ made (see 1 Ti 2:6 where the prepositional prefix to
this third word is *anti*); the basis is the blood of Christ (Heb
9:12); and the intended result is to purify a people zealous of
good works (Titus 2:14). Thus, the doctrine of redemption
means that because of the shedding of the blood of Christ,
believers have been purchased, removed from bondage, and
liberated.

It effected reconciliation. To reconcile means to change.
Reconciliation by the death of Christ means that man's
state of alienation from God is changed so that he is now
able to be saved (2 Co 5:19). When a man believes, then
his former state of alienation from God is changed into one of
being a member of His family. The extent of reconciliation
affects the entire world (2 Co 5:19) in the sense that trespasses are not imputed and God is able to offer man His love
in Jesus Christ; but it affects believers in a saving sense so
that when that gift of love is personally received we are
saved (Ro 5:11). The basis of reconciliation is the death
of Christ (Ro 5:11). It is important to observe that in reconciliation only man is changed — God is not; and, of course,
this makes sense — otherwise God would cease to be immutable and His holiness would be compromised. It is man who
needs changing, not God, and this is what happens in reconciliation.

It provides propitiation. To propitiate means to appease or
to satisfy a god. This naturally brings to mind the question,
Why does the deity need to be appeased? The biblical answer to that question is simply that the true God is angry
with mankind because of their sin. The theme of the wrath
of God appears throughout the Bible, including the teachings
of Christ (Mk 3:29; 14:21). Wrath is not merely the impersonal and inevitable working out of the law of cause and
effect, but it is a personal intervention of God in the affairs of
mankind (Ro 1:18; Eph 5:6).

The death of Christ propitiated God, averting His wrath and enabling Him to receive into His family those who place their faith in the one who satisfied Him. The extent of the propitiatory work of Christ is to the whole world (1 Jn 2:2), and the basis of propitiation is His shed blood (Ro 3:25).

Because Christ has died, God is satisfied. Therefore, we should not ask anyone to try to do anything to satisfy Him. This would mean trying to appease someone who is already appeased, which is totally unnecessary. Before the cross a person could not be certain that God was satisfied with whatever he brought to Him. That is why the publican prayed (literally) "God be propitiated toward me a sinner" (Lk 18:13). Today such a prayer would be a waste of breath, for God is propitiated by the death of Christ. Therefore, our message to men today should not suggest in any way that they can please God by doing something, but only that they be satisfied with the sacrifice of Christ which completely satisfied the wrath of God.

It judged the sin nature (Ro 6:1-10). The death of Christ had an important benefit for us in making inoperative the reigning power of our sin nature. Though this is not an easy concept to understand, Paul says that our union with Christ by baptism involves sharing His death so that we are dead to sin. The baptism must be that of the Holy Spirit, for no water, in whatever amount, could accomplish what is said to have been accomplished in this passage. The idea of death, so prominent in this passage, does not mean either extinction or cessation, but, as always, separation. Physical death, for unbeliever and believer alike, is neither extinction of that person nor cessation of activity, but separation of the spirit from the body. Spiritual death, the state of separation from God, is obviously not extinction or inactivity, for all unsaved people, who are very alive and active, are in this separated state. Even eternal death is not extinction, but separation forever from the presence of God in the lake of fire.

The crucifixion of the Christian with Christ means separa-

tion from the domination of sin over his life. The question in
verse 1, "Shall we continue in sin?" is answered by an em-
phatic *no* on the basis of our dying with Christ. This "destroyed" the body of sin. That word "destroy" does not mean
to annihilate, for if it did, then the sin nature would be eradicated, a fact which our experience with people scarcely con-
firms! It means to make the sin nature ineffective. The word
is used like this in 2 Thessalonians 2:8 of the man of sin who
is "destroyed" by the second coming of Christ but who continues to exist in the lake of fire without being annihilated
(Rev 20:10). But our crucifixion with Christ also means a
resurrection with Him to newness of living (Ro 6:4). Not
only has there been a separation from the old, but there is
also a new association with the resurrection life of Christ.
This is mentioned in every verse from 4 through 10. Union
with Christ, therefore, not only breaks the power of the old
capacity within us, but it also associates us with the risen
Christ, thus giving us the power to live according to the
dictates of the new capacity.

When did or does all this happen? Historically, it occurred when Christ died and rose again. As far as our personal history is concerned, this union with Christ does not
happen until we receive Him as Saviour and consequently
are at that moment baptized into His body by the Holy
Spirit. In other words, the historical actions of Christ's
death and resurrection become part of our personal history
when we believe.

Practically, of course, these truths may be present or absent from our daily experience. The fact that we have been
crucified with Christ and thus that the power of the sin nature has been broken and made inoperative is an unalterable
truth and does not depend on anything we do. But putting
this into practice does depend on yielding ourselves to His
control. For the Christian the sin nature is like a tyrant who
has been overthrown by the death of Christ. The believer is
therefore now free to live a life pleasing to God; and al-

though it is still possible to listen to and follow the prompt-
ings of sin, it will never be possible for sin to regain the
domination and control it had before conversion.

It brought the end of the law. The fact that the death of
Christ brought an end to the Mosaic law is quite clearly
stated in the New Testament (Ro 10:4; Col 2:14). The importance of this fact is related to (1) justification and (2)
sanctification, the former being much easier to see than the
latter. The reason is simply that the law could not justify a
sinner (Ac 13:39; Ro 3:20); therefore, if men are to be justified, another way must be provided. The law can show man
his need but it cannot provide the answer to that need (Gal
3:23-25). Thus the death of Christ opened the way for
justification of faith in Him alone.

But the relation of the end of the law to sanctification is
more difficult to comprehend simply because portions of the
Mosaic law are repeated in the New Testament in relation to
the believer's sanctification. Furthermore, those specifics
which are repeated are not from just one section of the law
(like the Ten Commandments). As a matter of fact, nine of
the Ten Commandments are repeated, and other parts of
the law are too (Ro 13:9). This makes it impossible to say
that the law is done away with except for the Decalogue.

Furthermore, 2 Corinthians 3:7-11 states quite clearly that
the Decalogue ("that which was written and engraven in
stones") was done away. How do you put all these facts together? Is the Christian under the Mosaic law in relation to
sanctification or not?

The only realistic solution that has ever appealed to the
present author is that which distinguishes a code and the
commandments contained in that code. The Mosaic law was
one of several codes which God has given throughout history, and as a code it is finished. The code under which the
believer lives today is called the law of Christ (Gal 6:2) or
the law of the Spirit of life (Ro 8:2).

As one code ends and another is instituted, not all of the

commands in the new one will themselves be new and different. The permission to eat meat in the law of Christ (1 Ti 4:3) was also part of the code under which Noah lived after the flood (Gen 9:3). Likewise, some of the specifics which were part of the Mosaic code have been incorporated into the law of Christ and some have not. But the entire code as a code has been done away with.

It is similar to the various codes in a household with growing children. At different stages of maturity new codes are instituted, but some of the same commandments often appear. To say that a former code with all of its commands is done away and to acknowledge that some of the same commands appear in a new code is no contradiction. It is as natural as growing up. But to grow up it is absolutely necessary to recognize that Christ's death did do away with the Mosaic law as a means of sanctification.

It is the ground for the believer's cleansing from sin (1 Jn 1:7). The blood (death) of Christ is the basis of our constant cleansing from sin. This does not mean that there is a recrucifixion or a dipping into blood with which to touch the erring Christian, but that the once-for-all death of our Lord provides constant cleansing when we sin as believers. Our family relationship is kept right by His death; our family fellowship is restored by our confession.

It is the basis for the removal of precross sins (Ac 17:30; Ro 3:25). Much about salvation in the Old Testament is not clear, but it does seem apparent that there was no final dealing with sin until the cross. Then all precross sins which were covered by sacrifices were taken away. The death of Christ is the basis for forgiveness in every age; faith is always the means. What we do not always know specifically is the particular content of faith that was required in each age.

It is the basis for the judgment of Satan and his demons (Col 2:15; Jn 12:31). Although Satan's judgments have and will occur in various stages, all are based on the victory which Christ won over him and his demons at the cross.

ITS ILLUSTRATIONS

Although there are numerous illustrations of the death of Christ in the Old Testament, the following are among the most prominent and worthy of detailed study: (1) the offering of Isaac by Abraham (Gen 22); (2) the Passover (Ex 12); (3) the five offerings of Leviticus 1–5; (4) the red heifer, an illustration of the continuous cleansing power of the death of Christ (Num 19); (5) the Day of Atonement (Lev 16); (6) the arrangement and service of the tabernacle.

ITS FALSE CONCEPTIONS

Throughout history men have come up with false ideas about the meaning of the death of Christ. Sometimes their ideas are completely false; at other times they have been partially true but inadequate because they omit the central idea of substitution.

1. *The death of Christ was a ransom paid to Satan.* While it is true that the Bible says His sacrifice paid a ransom, it does not say that it was paid to Satan.

2. *Christ's death was not necessary to pay for sin.* His death was simply an expression of the love of God which ought to exert a *moral influence* on us, softening our hearts and thus leading us to repentance.

3. *Christ's death did not atone for sin nor did it move God to pardon sin.* It reveals to men the way of faith and obedience as the way to eternal life and is thus an *example* to inspire us to lead a similar life.

4. *Christ died, an innocent victim, to satisfy the government of God since "public justice" must be upheld and the government of God vindicated.* His death demonstrated how the law regards sin.

5. *Modern, nonconservative theories of the atonement.* These regard Christ's death as having the elements of example, moral influence, and demonstration of God's hatred of sin and love for mankind, but they omit the basic concept of substitutionary sacrifice as the payment for sin.

ITS EXTENT

The question of the extent of the atonement — that is, did Christ die for all men or just for the elect—has been debated for centuries. Certain phrases in some verses might seem to limit the extent of the atonement, for example, "for the sheep" in John 10:15, "for the church" in Ephesians 5:25, "for many" in Matthew 20:28. But there are other passages which definitely seem to broaden the extent of the atonement to include all men. Notice especially John 1:29; 3:17; 2 Corinthians 5:19; 1 Timothy 4:10; 2 Peter 2:1; and 1 John 2:2. Of course, these unlimited verses can include the truth of the limited ones; but since the reverse is not true, it seems best to conclude that the death of Christ was unlimited in its value. It was for all men, but of course the personal application of that death is limited to those who believe in Him.

Some of the Benefits of Christ's Death

Among the almost innumerable blessings of salvation are many which are obvious to believers because they can be experienced, for example, prayer. But there are also many benefits which in themselves are not experienced (though their results are) and which are often not so well understood, for example, justification. And yet these are the bases for those experiences which are so vital to a normal Christian life.

THE DEATH OF CHRIST IS THE BASIS FOR
OUR ACCEPTANCE WITH GOD

That Christ's death makes us acceptable before God is expressed in such doctrines as redemption (Ro 3:24), reconciliation (2 Co 5:19-21), forgiveness (Ro 3:25), deliverance (Col 1:13), acceptance in the Beloved (Eph 1:6), assured future glorification (Ro 8:30), and justification (Ro 3:24).

Justification may need further elaboration. To justify is to declare one righteous. It is a judicial term indicating that a verdict of acquittal has been announced, and so excluding all possibility of condemnation. Indeed, in Scripture, justification is invariably set over against condemnation (Deu 25: 1; Ro 5:16; 8:33-34). Justification is always accomplished on a just basis, namely, that the claims of God's law against the sinner have been fully satisfied. Justification is not because of any overlooking, suspending or altering of God's righteous demands, but because in Christ all of His demands have been fulfilled. Christ's perfect life of obedience to the law and His atoning death which paid its penalty are the bases for our justification (Ro 5:9). Justification could never be based on our good works, for God requires perfect obedience and this is impossible for man.

The means of justification is faith (Ro 3:22, 25, 28, 30). Faith is never the ground of justification; it is the means or channel through which God's grace can impute to the believing sinner the righteousness of Christ. When we believe, all that Christ is, God puts to our account; thus we stand acquitted. Then God can justly announce that, acquittal, and that pronouncement is justification. The Bible never says we are justified on account of our faith — that would make faith a meritorious work and thus justification by works. Faith is like an outstretched empty hand which receives the righteousness of Christ. The believer is righteous because he is in Christ; God can announce that he is righteous, and that is justification.

BELIEVING IN CHRIST ALSO BRINGS A NEW POSITION

This includes citizenship in heaven (Phil 3:20), membership in a holy and royal priesthood (1 Pe 2:5, 9), membership in the family of God (Eph 2:19) by spiritual birth (Jn 3:5), marriage (Rev 19:7) and adoption (Gal 4:5).

Adoption is a particularly wonderful benefit of Christ's death for the believer. The doctrine is exclusively Pauline. Every time you read "son" in relation to a believer (not of Christ) in John's writings, for instance, you should translate it "child," for John does not write of the sonship of the

believer. Only Paul reveals that we are adopted as sons. It is
true that we are children of God by the new birth, but it is
also true that we are adopted into God's family at the same
time. In the act of adoption a child is taken by a man from
a family not his own, introduced into a new family, and regarded as a true son with all the privileges and responsibilities that belong to this new relationship. The imagery in the
idea of a child of God is one of birth, growth, development
into maturity; the idea in sonship is that of full-fledged privileges in the new family of God. Adoption bestows a new status on the one who receives Christ.

The results of adoption are deliverance from slavery, from
guardians, and from the flesh (Gal 4:1-5; Ro 8:14-17), and
it is the Holy Spirit who enables us to enjoy the privileges of
our position.

THE DEATH OF CHRIST GIVES THE BELIEVER AN INHERITANCE

This includes our being complete in Christ (Col 2:9-10),
possessing every spiritual blessing (Eph 1:3), and the assurance of heaven (1 Pe 1:4).

STRENGTH AND POWER TO LIVE THE CHRISTIAN LIFE
ARE ALSO ASSURED BY THE DEATH OF CHRIST

The blessings of salvation include being under grace (so
that we need not continue in sin, Ro 6:14), freedom from the
law (2 Co 3:6-13), and being indwelt by each Person of
the Godhead (Eph 4:6; Gal 2:20; 1 Co 6:19).

ANOTHER IMPORTANT BENEFIT OF THE DEATH OF
CHRIST IS SANCTIFICATION

The word *sanctify* means to set apart (it has the same root
as the words *saint* and *holy*). For the Christian, sanctification has three aspects. First, the believer has been set apart
by his position in the family of God. This is usually called
positional sanctification. It means being set apart as a member of the household of God. It is true of every believer

regardless of his spiritual condition, for this concerns his spiritual state. Read 1 Corinthians 6:11 and remember the carnal condition of these believers. That this positional sanctification is based on the death of Christ is clear from Hebrews 10:10.

Of course, there is also the experiential aspect of sanctification. Because we have been set apart we are to be increasingly set apart in our daily lives (1 Pe 1:16). In the positional sense no one is more sanctified than another, but in the experiential aspect it is quite correct to speak of one believer as being more sanctified than another. All the exhortations of the New Testament concerning spiritual growth are pertinent to this progressive and experiential facet of sanctification.

There is also a sense in which we will not be fully set apart to God until our position and practice are brought into perfect accord, and this will occur only when we see Christ and become as He is (1 Jn 3:1-3). Thus there is an aspect to sanctification which is often called ultimate or future sanctification and which awaits our complete glorification with resurrection bodies (Eph 5:26-27; Jude 24-25).

SECURITY OF THE BELIEVER

The question of eternal security must be thought of only in relation to a true believer. Of course, therein is the rub, for often it is difficult to tell if someone who may appear to reject the truth he once seemed to hold was ever genuinely saved. Also we know that there will be carnal Christians in heaven whose works have, for the most part, been wood, hay and stubble, but who, nevertheless, are saved (1 Co 3:15). To look at their lives would most likely lead to the conclusion that some of them, at least, had lost their salvation. But, these practical matters notwithstanding, the question of eternal security is still this: Can a true believer ever lose his salvation by either sinning or ceasing to believe or in any other way?

THE EVIDENCE FOR ETERNAL SECURITY

The doctrine of security, in the last analysis, depends on what God has done, so that if one can lose his salvation then certain works of God would have to be undone or reversed. For instance,

1. When we are saved the Holy Spirit places us in the body of Christ (1 Co 12:13). Now if a believer can lose his salvation, he would be removed from the body at that time; no such idea is even hinted at in the Scriptures.

2. Furthermore, the Holy Spirit seals the believer until the day of redemption (Eph 1:13; 4:30). Losing one's salvation would have to involve breaking that seal before the day of redemption.

3. Also, it is the Father's purpose to keep us in spite of everything (Jn 10:28-30; 13:1) and ultimately to present us faultless in His own presence (Jude 24).

4. But undoubtedly the most convincing Scripture reference about security is Romans 8:29-39. Notice the pileup of evidence. First, those who were predestinated, called and justified are also said to be glorified. The past tense can be used of a future event only because it is so certain that not one will be lost. The chain from foreknowing through predestinating, calling and justifying remains unbroken until all are glorified. Second, no one can charge God's elect with anything that could cause them to lose their salvation because the Judge (God) before whom such a charge would be tried is the same one who justifies (v. 33); that is, the Judge has already pronounced us righteous (to justify means to declare righteous). If anyone does bring a charge, what chance would he have of success when the accused has been declared righteous by the presiding Judge? Third, our Lord is continually making intercession for us, and that in itself is enough to keep us saved (v. 34, cf. 1 Jn 2:1). Fourth, the chapter closes with the certain and sweeping promise that nothing (including ourselves "nor any other [created thing]," v. 39) can separate us from the love of

God which is in Christ Jesus our Lord. That pretty well plugs every loophole!

Now, of course, people can and sometimes do believe the doctrine of eternal security and use it to allow themselves to live in sin without fear of losing their salvation. It should never be used that way; indeed, it ought to make us so grateful that we will want to live holy lives (Ro 6:1-14). But, like any truth, it can be falsified by perversion. Actually, one would not need to fear losing his salvation as long as he knew he could be saved again by believing again. So even a doctrine of "insecurity" could breed license in living.

SOME PROBLEM PASSAGES

Most of the problem passages which might seem to teach that there is no security were written in the context of practical problems in churches. Even in New Testament times it was hard to know which individuals were genuinely saved in a mixed church group, so sometimes a biblical writer would exhort some persons to produce evidence of their faith and others to be sure that they had exercised saving faith.

For example, Hebrews 6:4-6, though variously interpreted, is likely a warning to believers who were apparently content to remain in their state of immaturity. So, the writer says, let's go on to maturity (v. 1) because there is no way to start over in the Christian life. You can only stand still or go forward. If this passage were teaching that it is possible to lose one's salvation, then it also states in no uncertain terms that it is impossible to be saved a second time. Actually, then, it teaches too much for an "insecurity" position.[5]

John 15:6, in the author's judgment, is a reference to the burning of useless works at the judgment seat of Christ (as in 1 Co 3:15), but salvation is assured even though this happens. Many take these two passages as referring to those who merely made a profession of faith and who are not genuinely born again.

James 2:14-26 is saying that a nonworking faith is not the

kind of faith that saves in the first place. What is said in that passage is like a two-coupon train or bus ticket. One coupon says, "Not good if detached" and the other says, "Not good for passage." Works are not good for passage, but faith detached from works is not saving faith!

A book of this size cannot discuss every passage involved in this question. Good commentaries are readily available for further study.

THE TERMS OF SALVATION

More than 200 times in the New Testament, salvation is said to be conditioned solely on the basis of faith — faith that has as its object the Lord Jesus who died as our substitute for sin (Jn 3:16; Ac 16:31). Salvation is a free gift; therefore, any statement of the terms must carefully avoid implying that we give God something. He gives it all; we receive that gift through faith (Jn 1:12).

The preaching of any different gospel than that of salvation by grace through faith comes under the anathema of Galatians 1:8-9. This means an utter detesting because of the worthlessness of such a false gospel (later the word denoted excommunication). This is the strongest kind of warning that could be given, and yet through the centuries and in our own day there have been and are preached a number of false gospels.

BELIEVE AND SURRENDER

The question involved is simply this: Must there be a commitment to Christ as Lord of one's life in order to be saved? Many today are answering yes. For instance, a well-known author writing concerning erroneous ways of presenting the gospel asks, "Or will it leave them supposing that all they have to do is to trust Christ as a sin-bearer, not realizing that they must also deny themselves and enthrone Him as their Lord (the error which we might call only believism)?"[6] In other words, one must believe *and* give Christ control of his life in order to be saved. Sometimes it is said only that there must be a willingness to surrender even if the surrender of life does not occur. At least this would allow for the existence of carnal Christians (of which there seem to be plenty). But, if willingness is required at the moment of believing in order to be saved, how much willingness is necessary? Can, for instance, a man who is convinced in his mind that smoking is wrong (simply for medical reasons) not be saved until he is at least willing to give up his smoking? Or if surrender is necessary in order to be saved, why does the New Testament ask *believers* to surrender (Ro 12:1)?

The reasons for this viewpoint are at least four: (1) It is a sincere attempt to try to eliminate shallowness in professions of faith. (2) It does not understand the various meanings of the word *Lord*. (3) It is unclear on the concept of discipleship. (4) It attempts to counter "easy (or only) believism." But, of course, ultimately the matter can be decided only on the basis of what the Scriptures teach about believing and surrendering.

Shallowness is, of course, something the Lord Himself told us to expect when the Word is preached (Lk 8:12-15). Many cases of unyielded believers are evident in the letters to the seven churches in Revelation 2—3. (Note carefully, for instance, Rev 2:13-14; 2:19-20). Carnal believers whose lives will not merit reward will, nevertheless, be saved (1 Co 3: 15). Much as one might like to see the church free of false professors and shallow believers, this simply won't be possible according to the Bible.

The word *Lord* has various meanings. Sometimes it is simply a title of respect like our word *sir* (Jn 4:11). Sometimes it does mean Master (Lk 6:46). But usually in the New Testament it is the equivalent of the Old Testament name for God, *Yahweh*. When Jesus of Nazareth claimed to be God and when His followers assigned the title *Lord* to Him (Lord Jesus), this was a clear indication that He was Yahweh of the Old Testament incarnate in Jesus of Nazareth.

It was a claim to be the God-man. The people of His day would not have been concerned to stone Him or crucify Him if He had claimed merely to be Sir Jesus or Master Jesus, but when the claim was made for His being Yahweh Jesus, that put Him in an entirely different category. Now, of course, lordship in that sense of deity is absolutely essential to the work of salvation, for the Saviour must be a God-man in order to be able to save. He must be man to be able to die, and He must be God in order for that death to be an effective payment for sins. This is the meaning of Romans 10:9 and Acts 2:36.

A disciple is a learner, and there can be, like Judas, unsaved disciples of the Lord. Making disciples involves baptizing those who believe and teaching them continually (Mt 28:19). Confusion enters when we attempt to take the conditions for spiritual growth and make them conditions for becoming a disciple, or when we make the characteristics of the life of discipleship conditions for entering the life of a disciple. Notice carefully that the Lord distinguished these two aspects of discipleship in two side-by-side sermonettes. In Luke 14:16-24 He related the parable of the great supper into which entrance was unrestricted, free and for all. In Luke 14:25-33 He taught the restrictions of the life that continues to follow Him in the continuing process of discipleship, and they were very strict. To make these conditions for the life of service requirements for acquiring the life is to confuse the gospel utterly by muddying the clear waters of the grace of God with the works of man. Incidentally, it is worth noticing that the characteristics of discipleship require action, not merely the willingness to act!

Are there examples of uncommitted, unsurrendered though genuine believers in the Bible? Yes, there are. Lot, whom the New Testament calls "righteous" (2 Pe 2:7), is an example of lifelong rejection of God's lordship over his life. Peter gave an example of temporary rejection of the lordship of Christ when he said, "Not so, Lord" (Ac 10:14). Perhaps the clearest example is seen in the believers at Ephesus (Ac 19:8-19). Some had been saved for two years or longer before they brought their books of magic and burned them, confessing at the time that to have and use such books was a sin. In other words, there were people at Ephesus who accepted Christ as Saviour knowing that they should give up their use of magic but who did not give it up, some of them for as long as two years after they had become Christians; and yet their unwillingness to do · this did not prevent their becoming believers. Their salvation did not depend on faith plus willingness to surrender the use of magic.

Is it easy to believe? Not if you realize what is involved in that faith. For one thing, the object of our faith involves unbelievable demands because we ask people to believe a Person whom they've never seen nor has anyone else living today and the records of whom were written by His friends. Is it really easy to believe in an unseen Christ? For another thing, the content of our faith involves unbelievable demands. We ask people to trust this unseen Person about forgiveness of their sins and the issue of eternal life on the basis of the death of that Person which claims to be the payment for sin. Is that easy?

If you are ever tempted to add something to the uncomplicated grace of God (even out of good motives), first try making it crystal clear to people who the object of our faith is and what we are asking them to believe about Him. Then point men to Him, the Lord Jesus, the God-man Saviour who offers eternal life and forgiveness of sins to all who believe. This is what the Lord Himself did early in His ministry when He dealt with a sinner. He said to that Samaritan woman, "If thou knewest the gift of God, and who it is that saith to thee, Give me to drink; thou wouldest have asked of him, and he would have given thee living water" (Jn 4:10). All He asked of her was that she acknowledge Him as the Christ (v. 26) and receive the *gift* of eternal life from Him.

He did not tell her to straighten out the tangled affairs of her sinful life in order to be saved.

BELIEVE AND BE BAPTIZED

Baptism is an important God-given way of testifying to one's faith, but it is not a condition for being saved. You can get to heaven without being baptized (like the thief on the cross). Several verses are used by those who require baptism for salvation (and hundreds of other verses are ignored). Acts 2:38 may be translated, "Be baptized because of the remission of sins" — the preposition indicating the basis or ground rather than air or purpose (like "wanted for murder"). Though not the customary usage, it has to have that meaning in Matthew 12:41, for instance. The remission of sins, then, is the basis for being baptized and not the aim of baptism.[7]

Acts 22:16 seems to say that baptism washed away Paul's sins. However, when the verse is diagrammed it clearly does not say that. There are two imperatives (be baptized and wash) and two participles (having arisen and having called) in the verse and they pair off like this: arise, having been baptized; wash away your sins, having called on the Lord's name. In other words, the washing away of sins and the baptism are not connected as cause and effect. The arising is due to baptism having occurred, and the washing away of sin is due to having called on the Lord's name.

Mark 16:16 is not well attested by the best Greek manuscripts and was most likely not a part of the original writing of Mark. At best, it would be risky to build a doctrine of baptism necessary for salvation on such a debated text. If it is inspired, then it would be well for those who teach baptismal regeneration to notice that baptism is omitted from the last part of the verse. At best, the teaching that baptism is necessary to be saved is based on passages with debatable meanings. The clear statements of the Lord and the apostles require faith in Christ alone (Jn 6:29; Ac 13:39).

REPENT AND BELIEVE

To repent is to change your mind. However, this only defines the word, not the concept, for you need to ask, Change your mind about what? Depending on how you answer that question, repentance might be a synonymous concept to believing in Christ or it might become an additional requirement for salvation. If repentance is understood to mean changing your mind about your sin — being sorry for your sin — this will not necessarily save. There are plenty of criminals in and out of jails who are repentant in this sense. They are sorry for making certain mistakes, but this does not mean they give up a life of crime. People can be sorry for their sins without wanting to accept the forgiveness of a Saviour.

But if repentance means changing your mind about the particular sin of rejecting Christ, then that kind of repentance saves, and of course it is the same as faith in Christ. This is what Peter asked the crowd to do on the day of Pentecost. They were to change their minds about Jesus of Nazareth. Formerly they had considered Him to be only a blasphemous human being claiming to be God; now they changed their minds and saw Him as the God-man Saviour whom they would trust for salvation. That kind of repentance saves, and everyone who is saved has repented in that sense.

There is a third use of the concept of repentance and that is in the Christian life. A Christian needs to repent — that is, to change his mind about particular sins committed. If he does repent, then he will confess those sins and experience forgiveness.

Sometimes hymns and gospel songs express good theology and sometimes bad. But there is at least one song that does state clearly the requirement for being saved. It is, "Only Trust Him." That is exactly right. Faith is the *only* condition. Anything added becomes a work attached to the grace of God. *Faith* is the condition, and it is faith in *Him* who alone can save. This is the grace of God.

8

What Is the Church?

LAY CHRISTIANS, theologians, and churchmen all seem to be confused today about the church. Many believers know little more about the church than that it is their particular place of worship on such-and-such street. Theologians are confused about important matters, such as when the church began, and churchmen themselves are divided on matters of government, goals, and activities for the church. Added to all this is the suspicion that the church may have entirely lost its usefulness, and that we should use other agencies for doing the Lord's work.

To this last charge let it be said that God is not through with His church. No matter how heretical or worldly a church may be, Christ still seeks to work through it (Rev 2-3). The home and the church are the only two God-ordained "institutions" for carrying out His work. This is not to say that God does not use other organizations in His program, but it is to emphasize that the church is of primary importance in His purpose. When we abandon the church we abandon God's organization (1 Ti 3:15).

WHAT IS INCLUDED IN THE CONCEPT OF THE CHURCH?

The Greek word which we translate *church* is made up of two words which mean "to call out"; thus it comes to mean a gathering or assembly. But, like so many important words, it needs qualifying — an assembly of whom? (1) Sometimes it means (even in the New Testament) an assembly of townspeople, called out in a political gathering (Ac 19:32, 39, 41). (2) At least one time it refers to the gathering of the Jewish people in their assembling in the wilderness (Ac 7:38). (3)

140

Most frequently the word indicates a local group of Christians living in a certain place (1 Co 1:2; 1 Th 1:1; Rev 1:11 and many more). (4) The New Testament gives to this word a technical meaning when it refers to the church universal to which all believers and only believers belong; this is the same as the body of Christ (Mt 16:18; Eph 1:22-23; 3: 10, 21; 5:23, 25, 27, 29, 32; Col 1:18, Heb 12:23).

To summarize: the meaning of the word *church* is assembly. The kind of an assembly must be determined from the passage where the word is used. The doctrine of the Christian church is concerned only with uses (3) and (4) above.

THE LOCAL CHURCH

WHAT IS A LOCAL CHURCH?

There is a good deal of discussion today about what is necessary to constitute a local church. Is a church simply a gathering of two or three believers in the name of Christ? How much or how little organization is required? Is baptism necessary for church membership? Unfortunately the New Testament does not provide a formal definition of a local church, but it does describe the normal features of a functioning local assembly. And it is from these regular characteristics of local churches that we can formulate at least a descriptive definition. Taking together the features of local churches we see in the New Testament, we might propose the following definition: A local church is an assembly of professing believers in Christ who have been baptized and who are organized to do God's will. Notice: (1) There must be a profession of faith — not just anyone can belong to a local church. (2) The New Testament knows nothing of unbaptized church members. (3) Churches were always organized as soon as possible (Ac 14:23) — an informal, unorganized fellowship of believers does not constitute a church. (4) There is purpose — doing God's will which is expressed in many ways (like observing the ordinances, being open and available for ministry to all age groups in all parts of the world, etc.)

If this be a reasonably good working definition of the local church, then two or three gathered for fellowship is not a local church since such assemblies are generally not organized nor anxious to minister to all age groups even in their own neighborhoods. Furthermore, a Christian school or extra-church Christian organization does not qualify because of its selective ministry; that is, all professing believers would not be permitted to associate with the institution or organization. Can you imagine a Christian school throwing open its doors to all without any admission requirements? Or can you imagine the problems a youth work would have if retirees could freely enter into its activities? Have you noticed that often today the criticism of the church is coming from those who are associated with organizations whose work would be seriously affected if they had to open their doors to everybody? Naturally, you can be more effective and "successful" if you can be selective, but if you have to receive and try to help people without restrictions, then, like some local churches, you won't always be successful.

Of course, this definition does allow for some flexibility. It does not require that a local church meet in a building specially set aside for such a purpose. It does not indicate what kind of or how many meetings are required to constitute a church. Actually it does not specify the mode of baptism or the particular kind of officers (though perhaps it could and should — more of that later). Principally it tries to differentiate the local church from other groups, even church-related ones.

WHO ARE THE LEADERS OF THE CHURCH?

That the church is to have leadership is a divine requirement (Heb 13:7, 17). Organization is not wrong or carnal. People go to extremes on this matter. Some feel that the less organization the better, though in practice the work is hindered by not having sufficient organization. Others go to the other extreme and are so highly organized that it is difficult, if not impossible, for the Head of the church to be heard. Nevertheless, the New Testament does sanction several classes of leaders.

1. Elders. Without doubt elders were the principal leaders of New Testament churches. Though all do not agree, it appears that elders and bishops occupied the same position in the church — the term *elder* emphasizing more the office and the term *bishop* emphasizing more the function of that office, namely, general oversight. At least in Ephesus these were the same (Ac 20:17, 28). In addition to general oversight of the work, elders ruled (1 Ti 5:17), guarded and taught the truth (Titus 1:9) and supervised financial matters (Ac 11:30). The question of how many elders there were in each assembly is debated. Clearly there were several elders in each city where there were churches (Ac 14:23; Phil 1:1), but whether this meant several elders in each house church or possibly one elder in each individual congregation (and thus a plurality in each city) is debatable. Notice 1 Timothy 3 where the bishop (singular) is spoken of in verses 1-7; then the deacons (plural) are described in verses 8-13. Elders were apparently ordained or set aside for their special ministry in the church (1 Ti 4:14; Titus 1:5).

The qualifications for the elders are spelled out in great detail in 1 Timothy 3:1-7 and Titus 1:5-9. The former passage (which is the more detailed one) lists them as follows: blameless (not open to criticism), husband of one wife (may mean only one wife ever, since the Greek is the same as in 1 Ti 5:9 and since polygamy was unknown among the Greeks and Romans, or it may bar those who remarry after divorce), vigilant (steady, calm), sober (sound-minded), good behavior, hospitable, apt to teach, not given to wine, no striker (no physical violence), not money mad, patient (not determined to have his just due), no brawler (not contentious), not covetous, presiding well over his family (the small circle of the home is a test for how well he will rule in the church), not a novice (not a new, immature convert), having a good testimony among the unsaved in the community. The passage in Titus adds: not self-willed (not arrogant), not soon angry (not hot-headed), lover of good (people and things), just (upright), holy (pure), and temperate (self-controlled).

The significance of such a great amount of detail should not be missed. It seems to be saying that it is exceedingly important to have qualified men to lead the church, and that it is better to have fewer elders who are qualified than a larger number, some of whom are not qualified.

2. *Subordinate to the elders were the deacons.* The word *deacon* means servant; while all Christians can serve, certain ones were officially recognized in New Testament times as appointed servants to the church. Though helpers of the elders (Ac 6:1-6), they were an officially recognized group (Phil 1:1). The qualifications for deacons, though not so detailed as for the elders, did include some of the same requirements. In addition it is stated that deacons are not to be "doubletongued" (1 Ti 3:8). This might indicate that deacons had more face-to-face and house-to-house contact with members of the local group in administering relief aid or visiting the sick, so they had to be reminded to be especially careful not to say one thing to one person and another thing to another. The fact that deacons are not mentioned in the parallel passage in Titus 1 does not indicate that they were optional at all. It may indicate either that the churches in Crete were not large enough yet to require more than elders to lead them, or it may mean that they had deacons but were lacking in elders.

3. *Deaconesses?* Only two verses in the New Testament might possibly support the existence of deaconesses in those days. In Romans 16:2, Phoebe is called a "servant" (the word is *deacon*). The question is whether this is an official (deaconess) or unofficial (servant) use of the word. Probably it is unofficial (as in 1 Co 16:15). The other relevant verse is 1 Timothy 3:11 where certain women are mentioned.

The question is whether these are the wives of the deacons or deaconesses (the word in the original is simply that for women). If they were deaconesses one would expect that they would be mentioned after verse 13 when the discussion of the deacons was finished rather than inserted right in the middle of the paragraph about deacons. That seems to point to the conclusion that they were the wives of the deacons. It is highly doubtful that there was an office of deaconess in the early church.[1]

4. *Of course there was no such office as that of trustee in the New Testament.* And yet churches find it necessary to have such people today in order to hold the property in the name of the group. New Testament churches meeting in homes did not hold property in the name of the group; today's churches meeting in their own buildings should not hold their properties in the names of individuals. Hence, the need for trustees today. By the way, 2 Corinthians 8:17-24 mentions a group of trustees of money. Of course the need for trustees during the first century when the church was not a legal institution is quite different from the current situation.

We have been discussing officers or leaders in the church, but it is important to remember that the ministry of the church is not carried on solely by them. They govern, guide, guard and minister, but other gifted people share in the actual ministry of a local assembly. There may be those with the gift of teaching who are not elders or deacons. Certainly helping, showing mercy, giving and other gifts are not limited in their distribution to those who occupy the offices in the congregation. Nevertheless, it is true that the leaders do share in the ministry through the use of their own spiritual gifts.

The question that always arises is simply this: How bound are we today to follow the leadership pattern of the New Testament? Obviously not all agree even on what the pattern is, or how closely it can be followed. The debate has

been going on for centuries and won't be settled in anybody's lifetime! Wouldn't a good procedure be something
like this: (1) try to ascertain as closely as possible what the
New Testament pattern is, then (2) work toward that ideal
in whatever situation you find yourself? There seems to be
little justification for going away from the New Testament
pattern; on the other hand, it may not be possible to put it
into practice in every detail in every situation.

HOW SHOULD A CHURCH BE GOVERNED?

Like the matter of officers, the question of government is
debated. The best we can do in a handbook like this is to
explain the various types of church government that are followed today.

The hierarchial forms of government. In this system
(practiced in varying ways by the Roman Catholic, Episco-
pal, Lutheran and Methodist churches) the bishops govern
the church (though there are also elders and deacons). Bishops alone have the power to ordain; and although this form
of government is not found in the New Testament, it did
arise in the second century.

The federal form of government. In this setup the church
is governed by the elders (as in the Presbyterian and some
independent churches) who are given their authority by the
congregation. It is a representative form of government in
which the people govern, not directly, but through their
representatives, the elders. Often a distinction is made between ruling elders (those who govern but do not preach
or administer the ordinances) and teaching elders (those
who preach and administer the ordinances) (1 Ti 5:17).

Arguments in support of the federal type include the fact
that elders were appointed by the apostles (Ac 14:23; Titus
1:5), there were obviously rulers over the churches besides
the apostles (Heb 13:7, 17), in matters of discipline the
leaders gave instructions as to what to do (1 Co 5; 1 Ti 5:
20), and ordination passages imply the federal system.

The congregational form of government. Followers of this polity believe that no man or group of men should exercise authority over a local assembly; therefore, the government should be in the hands of the members themselves. Baptists, Evangelical Free, Disciples, and some Bible and independent churches follow this pattern. Usually the officers of such churches are pastors and deacons. The pastor (usually only one in each church) is ordained to administer the ordinances and is often regarded as equivalent to the New Testament elder. Deacons (usually several in each church) are assigned the responsibility of supervising the welfare of the church. Some groups ordain deacons but do not permit them to administer the ordinances. Both pastor and deacons are chosen by vote of the entire congregation, and almost all the particular decisions affecting the life of the church are decided by the congregation (though implemented by the leaders).

Arguments in favor of this form of government include the many passages that speak of the responsibilities of the entire church (1 Co 1:10; Phil 1:27), the passages which seem to commit the ordinances of the church to the entire group, not just leaders (Mt 28:19-20; 1 Co 11:2, 20), the apparent involvement of the whole church in choosing leaders (Ac 6: 3, 5; 15:2, 30; 2 Co 8:19), and the fact that the whole church was involved in exercising discipline (Mt 18:17; 1 Co 5; 2 Th 3:14 f.).

Under the congregational system, the pastor is usually considered to be the single elder in the church. This is supported by the fact that the seven churches of Revelation 2 and 3 apparently had a single leader (called the "angel" but referring to the human leader), and by the fact that in 1 Timothy 3 the first part of the passage speaks of *the* bishop (elder) while the latter part (vv. 8-13) mentions the deacons. This would seem to indicate that there was only one elder in each church although there were several deacons. Those who favor the federal system point to the mention of elders and deacons (both in the plural) in such a passage as Philippians 1:1, which argues for elders and deacons in each local church.

The national church. In some countries, especially Europe, the head of the state is also the head of the church and leaders in the church are appointed by some agency of the state. This is true of the Lutheran Church in Scandinavia and of the Church of England.

No government. Probably there really isn't any church that practices this in reality, but some claim to be governed by no human beings, only by Christ the Head. In practice, however, human leaders often play a very decisive role in administering the affairs of the assembly.

Which form is the correct one? That's a question that has been debated ever since the earliest days of the church, so it will not be settled easily. Obviously the church did have government, and so no government does not follow the scriptural pattern. Equally apparent is the fact that the church and the Roman state were entirely separate in New Testament times. It is also true that the hierarchical church was a development in postbiblical times. So the federal or congregational forms of government are the only ones that can lay claim to being biblical at all. And perhaps rather than saying federal *or* congregational, one should say federal *and* congregational, for elements of both polities appear in the New Testament. Of course, a church cannot be completely governed by the congregation and be structured federally at the same time, but a church can have the federal structure with certain matters being decided by the congregation.

THE ORDINANCES OF THE CHURCH

Although ordinance and sacrament are listed as synonyms in the dictionary, there are some practical theological differences in what they connote. Sacrament usually has the idea of conveying grace automatically to the one partaking of the sacrament. Indeed, the Roman Catholic Council of Trent said, "A sacrament is something presented to the senses, which has the power, by divine institution, not only of signifying, but also of efficiently conveying grace." Ordinance, on the other hand, though variously defined, usually does not include the concept of effectively conveying grace to the participant. Using the basic idea in ordinance of "prescribed rite or practice," a working definition of an ecclesiastical ordinance might be "an outward rite prescribed by Christ to be performed by His church." Such a definition would reduce the possible number of ordinances to two — baptism and the Lord's Supper. It would eliminate, for instance, marriage (though often called an ordinance) simply because it was prescribed long before Christ. At any rate, without quibbling over the word itself, all we need to discuss here are those two ordinances which all agree are the principal ones.

The Lord's Supper. Various groups hold to different meanings for the Lord's Supper. The Roman Catholics teach that the bread and wine become the actual body and blood of Christ, though they obviously do not change their appearance. This view is called *transubstantiation* and is definitely unscriptural because it includes the idea that the body and blood of Christ are offered every time the mass is celebrated. In contrast to this, the Bible clearly and emphatically states that His death was complete, effective, and once for all (Heb 10:10; 9:12). Lutherans hold that the participant partakes of the true body and blood of Christ "in, with and under" the bread and wine, though there is no change in the elements at all. This many called *consubstantiation*. Others believe (and I think correctly) that the supper is strictly a memorial (1 Co 11:24-25 — "in remembrance"), the elements being unchanged and Christ present in the service but not in the elements in any way.

There are several purposes served in observing the Lord's Supper:

1. It is a remembrance of the life and death of our Lord. The bread symbolizes His perfect life, which qualified Him to be an acceptable sacrifice for sin, and the body in which He actually bore our sin on the cross (1 Pe 2:24). The wine represents His blood shed for the remission of our sins. We can never anticipate seeing that body again or another shedding of His blood, so this has to be a remembrance.

2. The supper is an announcing of these basic facts of the gospel (1 Co 11:26).

3. The supper serves to quicken our anticipation of His second coming, for we are reminded that we observe it only until He comes again (1 Co 11:26).

4. The supper should remind us of our oneness with each other in the body of Christ and of the fellowship which we share as fellow members of that body (1 Co 10:17).

How often should the Lord's Supper be observed? Some churches do it every three months and usually precede it by a preparation service sometime during the week before the Sunday it will be observed. Others do it once every month, while some feel it should be observed every Sunday. Actually the Scriptures do not clearly specify the exact frequency of taking the Lord's Supper. Although the first believers apparently did it daily immediately following Pentecost, this does not mean that it was observed in every house gathering every day but only daily somewhere in the city of Jerusalem (Ac 2:46). At Troas (Ac 20:7) it was observed on Sunday, but the text does not explicitly state that it was done every Sunday, though such a conclusion would be easily inferred from the passage. But however frequently it is done, it might be well to observe it sometimes in the evening service — not only because it was a supper, but also because this allows those who may be prevented from coming to a morning observance to participate on a regular basis. Since it is one of the most important things a church does, it should always be given ample time and never "tacked on" and rushed through.

Baptism. The matter of water baptism involves two questions: How should it be done (mode) and on whom should it be performed (subjects — believers only or also infants). But before plunging into those questions, a word might be in order about the meaning and importance of baptism.

Any definition of baptism will have to be broad enough to include its use in relation not only to Christian baptism but also Jewish proselyte baptism, Spirit baptism, and even that rather strange use in 1 Corinthians 10:2. Most definitions are constructed in terms of the etymological idea of immerse or submerge, but a theological definition of baptism would best be understood in terms of identification or association with something like a group or message or experience. This idea will fit the varied uses of baptism without injecting the question of mode.

Nonetheless, the mode of baptism has been and continues to be a much-debated question. Arguments for nonimmersion include the following:

1. The Greek word *baptizo* has a secondary meaning which means "to bring under the influence of," and of course pouring or sprinkling better pictures coming upon than immersion.

2. Indeed, if baptism illustrates the Spirit's coming upon a person, then pouring or sprinkling water on the top of the head best pictures this.

3. Immersion would have been highly improbable, if not impossible, in instances like those recorded in Acts 2:41 (too many people involved for immersion), Acts 8:38 (too little water available in a desert place), and Acts 10:47 and 16: 33 (not enough water in a house for immersion).

4. In Hebrews 9:10 the word *baptism* is used to include all sorts of Old Testament rituals, even those which involved sprinkling; thus the word does not always mean immerse exclusively.

5. The Greek language has an unmistakably clear word that means *dip*. Why isn't that used if this is the correct mode of baptism?

Arguments for immersion include the following:

1. Immerse is the primary meaning of the Greek word *baptizo.*

2. The normal understanding of the prepositions "into" and "out of" (the water) would indicate that immersion was practiced.

3. The baptism practiced on a proselyte to Judaism was a total immersion (though self-performed, not by another), and this would indicate that Christian baptism followed the same customary mode (though performed by another on the one being baptized).[2]

4. Immersion best pictures the significance of baptism which is death to the old life and resurrection to the new (Ro 6:1-4).

5. Immersion was the universal practice of the early church and every instance in the New Testament either demands or permits it (3,000 people could have been baptized in the various pools around Jerusalem on the day of Pentecost.

6. The Greek language has words for pour and sprinkle but these are never used of baptism.

One seems driven to the conclusion that immersion is the biblical mode. Immersion seems to have been the mode of baptism practiced universally in the early church. This is the most natural meaning of the word used and of the picture conveyed by the ordinance. The first exception to immersion was pouring, not sprinkling, and it was allowed in cases that could not be immersed such as sick people. Indeed, pouring was called "clinical baptism." Cyprian (A.D. 200-257) was evidently the first to approve of sprinkling, though it was not generally practiced until the twelfth century.

The other question concerns the proper subjects for baptism — believers only or should infants also be baptized? The arguments for infant baptism include:

1. The analogy between circumcision (which obviously was done on infants) as the initiatory rite into the old cove-

nant and baptism into the new.

2. Baptisms of entire households would certainly have included infants (as in Ac 16:33).

3. The New Testament seems to make promises to households where there is at least one believing parent; therefore, to baptize the infants in such households is quite proper (1 Co 7:14).

Arguments against infant baptism and for believers' baptism include:

1. If baptism is an initiatory rite it must only be performed on those who have exercised faith in Christ and thus have been made members of God's family. Only natural birth was necessary to become a member of Israel; but since the new birth is required to be a member of God's family today, then only those who can consciously exercise faith should be baptized.

2. Household baptisms in the New Testament do not specify the presence of infants.

3. There is no decisive evidence for the practice of infant baptism either by the Jews or Christians in apostolic times. If baptism is the sign of association with Christ and Christianity, then the sign should only be used by those who have so associated. And since the only way to associate is through the personal act of faith in Him, then baptism can only be properly experienced by those who have believed. It is clear, for instance, that all in the household of the Philippian jailor were of sufficient age to be able to hear and understand the word of the Lord which Paul preached to them (Ac 16:32). Thus those who believed and were baptized had reached an age of being able to understand intelligently. This may have included children, but not infants.

What about rebaptism? There is one clear example in the New Testament of such, and that is of the baptized disciples of John the Baptist who were later baptized with Christian baptism after hearing and responding to the Christian message as preached to them by Paul (Ac 19:1-7). This incident shows that John the Baptist's baptism and Christian baptism were not identical, and that even though one has been baptized before, when he becomes a believer in Christ he should be baptized again as a testimony of his identification with the new message and group.

What does Christ expect of the church? While there may be many ways such a question could be answered, here are a few suggestions:

1. The local church should always show its love for the Lord (Rev 2:4).

2. The church should minister to its own members so that they incite one another to love and good works (Heb 10:24).

3. The church is the agency for carrying out the Great Commission. While witnessing and teaching obviously can and should be done by individuals, these are also functions of the local church. The gospel should be preached in the services of the church so that when unbelievers come in they can hear it (1 Co 14:24), and all the epistles bear testimony to the teaching ministry of the local congregation.

4. The church is to care for its own who are in need, such as widows and orphans and the poor (Ja 1:27; 1 Ti 5:1-16; 2 Co 8–9).

5. The church is to do good in this world (Gal 6:10).

6. But basically the purpose of the church is to produce mature, stable, holy Christians. Doing this will sometimes involve discipline in the realm of morals (1 Co 5) and maintenance of purity in doctrine (2 Ti 2:16-18).

THE UNIVERSAL CHURCH

The universal church is that spiritual organism of which Christ is the Head and believers from Pentecost to the rap-

ture are the members. It is Christ's church in that He
claimed it as His (Mt 16:18). He taught those who would
first lead it (Jn 14–16), and was the one who sent the
Holy Spirit on the day of Pentecost to form it and empower
it (Ac 2:33). In His resurrection and ascension He became
Head over His body, the church (Eph 1:20-23), giving her
gifts (Eph 4:8-11) and preparing her to be His bride without spot and blemish (Eph 5:26-27).

Several important interpretive problems arise in connection with Christ's original prediction concerning the church
(Mt 16:18-19). One is, what is the rock on which He builds
it (v. 18)? The Roman Catholic Church answers that it is
Peter himself, a view which is untenable simply on the
grounds that the name Peter is masculine and the word for
rock is feminine. Even Peter admits that Christ is the rock,
not himself, on which the church is built (1 Pe 2:4-8). This
would seem to support the interpretation that the rock is
Christ (see also 1 Co 3:11), or perhaps the confession of
Christ as Peter made on that occasion and as every person
must make who becomes a member of Christ's church.

The other problem concerns the power of the disciples to
bind and loose (Mt 16:19). Notice it is things, not people,
over which they were given this power, and the text says
literally, "Whatsoever things you bind on the earth shall
have already been bound in heaven" and the same for loos-
ing. The same translation applies to similar words in John
20:23 in connection with forgiving and retaining sins. The
point in both verses is not that the disciples have inherent
power to bind, loose, forgive and retain, but they announce
or attest to what has already been done in heaven. God
initiates these things and the apostles announce them. An
example of things bound may be the things which the apostles bound on the church in Acts 15. An example of sins
retained may be in Acts 5:1-11. Although there may be
similarities in the responsibilities of church leaders today,
these prerogatives may have been exclusive with the apostles.

SOME ILLUSTRATIONS OF THE UNIVERSAL CHURCH

The relationships between Christ and His church are illustrated in a number of intriguing figures in the New Testament. Each one is worthy of detailed study, though we can only mention them here.

1. Christ is the Shepherd and we are His sheep (Jn 10). His care for us and our security in Him are the salient features of this illustration.

2. Christ is the vine and we are the branches (Jn 15). Fruitfulness comes only as we draw strength from the vine.

3. Christ is the cornerstone and we are the stones in the building (Eph 2:19-21). A cornerstone gives direction to the entire building and is, of course, laid only once.

4. Christ is the High Priest and we are a kingdom of priests (1 Pe 2). As priests we can offer ourselves, our substance and our service (Ro 12:1; Heb 13:15-16).

5. Christ is the Head and we are the members of His body (1 Co 12). As Head He directs; as members we serve each other through the exercise of the spiritual gifts which He as risen Head gives.

6. Christ is the last Adam and we are the new creation (1 Co 15:45). By faith we are placed in Christ, the last Adam, to partake of His resurrection life and power (Ro 5:19).

7. Christ is the Bridegroom and we are His bride (Eph 5:25-33; Rev 19:7-8). Everlasting love and the intimacy of the relationship of bridegroom and bride are the obvious points of this illustration.

8. Christ is the Heir and we are joint-heirs (Heb 1:2; Ro 8:17). This assures us of sharing in all the glories which shall be His when the world acknowledges Him.

9. Christ is the firstfruits and we are the harvest (1 Co 15:23). His resurrection guarantees ours.

10. He is the Master and we are His servants (Col 4:1; 1 Co 7:22). The servant does the will of his master, and in turn the master binds himself to take care of the servant.

WHEN DID THE CHURCH HAVE ITS BEGINNING?

A basic question which divides theologies is when the church began. What is known as covenant theology states that the church began in the Old Testament (usually with Abraham) and continues throughout all time. Thus the universal church, according to this viewpoint, consists of all believers of all time (or at least from Abraham on). Some groups believe that the church began with John the Baptist, simply because he apparently was the first man to baptize other people (other Jewish baptisms were self-administered) and baptism is the distinguishing feature of the church. Thus the church began with the first baptizer. A third group teaches that the church began on the day of Pentecost and consists of all believers of the present age. Still others hold that the body of Christ did not begin until sometime during the ministry of the apostle Paul (either at his conversion, or during the first missionary journey, or during his first confinement in Rome — that is, either at Ac 9, 13, or 28). Before that (from Pentecost until Ac 9, 13 or 28) there was a Jewish church but not the body church. So this is a rather decisive and devisive question.

That the day of Pentecost marked the beginning of the church seems evident for the following reasons:

1. The Lord spoke of the church as being future in Matthew 16:18. This apparently means that the church did not exist in Old Testament times.

2. The resurrection and ascension of Christ are essential to the functioning of the church. It is built on the resurrection (Eph 1:19-20), and the giving of gifts is required for its operation, which giving of gifts in turn is dependent on Christ's being ascended (Eph 4:7-12). If by some stretch of imaginative theology the body of Christ could be said to have been in existence before the ascension of Christ, then it will have to be concluded that it was an ungifted and inoperative body. The church's being built on the resurrection and ascension of Christ makes it distinctive to this age.

3. But the principal evidence that the church began on

158 A Survey of Bible Doctrine

the day of Pentecost concerns the baptizing work of the Holy Spirit. The Lord declared that this particular and distinctive ministry of the Spirit was still future just before His ascension (Ac 1:5). On the day of Pentecost it first occurred (the record does not say so in Ac 2 but it does in Ac 11:15-16). Now, what is it that Spirit baptism does? The answer to this is found in 1 Corinthians 12:13: it places the believer in the body of Christ. Since this is the only way to enter the body (i..e., by the baptizing work of the Spirit), and since this work of the Spirit first occurred on the day of Pentecost, then the conclusion seems obvious that the church, the body of Christ, began on the day of Pentecost.

WHEN WILL THE CHURCH BE COMPLETED?

If the church, the body of Christ, began at Pentecost, then to say that it will be completed at the rapture when the Lord calls it to Himself is not to say that there will not be others saved after that event. Just as there were redeemed Israelites before the day of Pentecost so there will be redeemed people after the rapture of the church, both during the tribulation period and the millennium. But though redeemed and assured of heaven, they will apparently not be a part of the body of Christ, which will be distinct from other redeemed people.

The heavenly Jerusalem, we are told, is inhabited by angels, the church, God, Jesus and "the spirits of just men made perfect" (apparently a reference to Old Testament saints). The point is, however, that there are distinct groups of believers in heaven. Distinction is maintained even though the destiny is the same.

It is also significant that the baptizing work of the Holy Spirit is nowhere mentioned as occurring during the tribulation or the millennium. This, too, would seem to point to the completion of the body of Christ before the tribulation will begin.

9

What Does the Future Hold?

MAN'S INTEREST in the future is legendary, and many prophets — true and false — have tried to satisfy that interest. Prophesying is a risky business, simply because you can't stay in business if you have too many failures. The Old Testament commanded that a prophet who failed to speak in the name of the Lord or whose prophecy failed to come to pass should be stoned without mercy (Deu 13:1-11; 18: 20-22). In the case of false prophets who might sometimes make accurate predictions (which occasionally happens even today), their message was to be measured against the true commands of the Lord previously given to His people. If they did not measure up, then those prophets were to be stoned also. The Bible, of course, not only contains many prophecies, but through its own prophecies gives assurance of their accuracy. Enough time has elapsed so that many of its predictions can be observed to have been fulfilled accurately, thereby giving assurance that those yet unfulfilled will come to pass exactly as recorded.

BASIC VIEWPOINTS CONCERNING THE FUTURE

It goes without saying that all are not agreed on the outline of the future. As a result there have developed in the Christian church three basic viewpoints concerning the interpretation of prophecy. They are all related to God's covenants with the Jewish people and especially to the covenant made with Abraham.

God's covenant with Abraham (Gen 12:1-3) was later confirmed and amplified (Gen 13:14-17; 15:1-7; 17:1-18).

In it were personal promises to Abraham himself that he would be specially blessed in temporal and spiritual things. These, of course, were fulfilled, for he acquired land, servants, cattle, silver and gold (Gen 13:14-15, 17; 15:7; 24:34-35); and he enjoyed communion with God and was called the friend of God (Gen 18:17; Ja 2:23). These predictions came true exactly as promised.

Promises were also made in that covenant to Abraham's descendants, the nation of Israel. For one thing, God promised to continue the covenant with Abraham's children (Gen 17:7), making them a great and innumerable nation (Gen 12:2; 13:16; 15:5). But most interesting in the light of current events was the promise to give Abraham's descendants, the Jewish people, a particular piece of land whose boundaries were clearly specified for an everlasting possession (Gen 15:18; 17:8).

In the covenant, too, was a promise that concerned all people; namely, that those who blessed Abraham and his descendants would be blessed, and those who cursed them would be cursed. This principle operated during Abraham's lifetime (Gen 14:12-20; 20:2-18), during the experiences of the children of Israel (Deu 30:7; Is 14:1-2) and will operate during the tribulation period (Mt 25:40). There was also a promise that in Abraham all the families of the earth would be blessed. This has been fulfilled in God's using Israel as the channel for giving us the Bible and in sending Christ as *the* Seed of Abraham (Gal 3:16).

All agree that many of these promises made to Abraham in the covenant have been literally fulfilled. But the promise concerning the occupancy of the land has not been fulfilled, at least not literally. The boundaries were stated as being "from the river of Egypt unto the great river, the river Euphrates" (Gen 15:18). All agree that the eastern boundary is the river Euphrates. Not all agree what is meant by the river of Egypt. Some think it is a reference to the Nile and others relate it to the Wady-el-Arish, not far from Gaza. In either case Israel has not in all her history, nor yet today, occupied the land according to these boundaries.

One of the major questions concerning the Abrahamic covenant is whether its promises are conditioned on obedience or whether they are unconditional. If they were conditioned on the Jews' faithfulness or goodness, then we may safely assume that all claims to Palestine and other blessings included in the covenant have been forfeited, for certainly the Jewish people have sinned repeatedly. If, on the other hand, the promises were conditioned only on God's faithfulness, they must be fulfilled in spite of man's unfaithfulness.

The answer to this question of conditionality or unconditionality is found in an action God took to confirm the covenant that is recorded in Genesis 15:9-17. The Lord solemnized the covenant in the recognized way by sacrificing animals and laying the severed parts on the ground. Ordinarily the two parties to the agreement would walk together between the parts of the sacrifice, but on this occasion there was a striking exception. Instead of both God and Abraham walking between the pieces of the sacrifice, God put Abraham to sleep and passed alone between the parts of the animals. God could hardly have demonstrated more clearly that the keeping of this covenant depended on Him alone.

Furthermore, the covenant was reaffirmed to Abraham's son, Isaac, and to Isaac's son Jacob (Gen 26:2-4; 28:13-15). No conditions were attached in either instance, and the reaffirmation was made on the basis of the oath with which God made the covenant with Abraham originally. In addition, it is apparent that Abraham sinned during the years between the making of the covenant and its confirmation to Isaac; so if God had viewed the covenant as conditioned on obedience, He would have had to nullify it because Abraham had been disobedient (Gen 12:10-20). To be sure, some contingencies are involved in the *intermediate* fulfillments of aspects of the covenant, but the *ultimate* fulfillment is unconditioned. Throughout Israel's history, obedience was God's condition for possessing the land even temporarily and partially, and dispersion was the judgment for disobedience (Deu 28:25; Jer 25:11). However, the ultimate and full fulfillment will be brought about by God, and Israel will then be converted and obedient under the reign of Messiah.

To David and his descendants God also made some important promises in the Davidic covenant (2 Sa 7:12-16). He promised that Solomon, not David, would build the temple, and that David's lineage, throne and kingdom would be established forever. All agree that Christ is the Seed of David who is the ultimate Fulfiller of the promise, for Luke 1:32-33 designates Him as such. These promises concerning the King and the kingdom were often repeated in the Old Testament, the most forceful statement being in Psalm 89 where the Lord warned of chastisement for disobedience but said that the covenant would not be broken or altered in any way (vv. 30-37). Other relevant passages are Isaiah 9: 6-7, Jeremiah 23:5-6, Ezekiel 37:24-25, Hosea 3:4-5, Amos 9:11 and Zechariah 14:4-9. Though all agree that Christ is the one who fulfills this covenant, not all agree on *when* He does. Is He now sitting on the throne of David in heaven? Is the kingdom the church? Or is all of this yet future when Christ will rule over a kingdom on earth? The answers to these questions are the bases for the different viewpoints concerning the picture of the future. The three basically different millennial viewpoints are based on the questions of the unconditional or conditional nature of the Abrahamic covenant and the fulfillment of the kingdom promises of the Davidic covenant.

POSTMILLENNIALISM

This viewpoint teaches that the second coming of Christ will occur *after* (post) the millennium. Postmillennialists look for a utopian state on earth to be brought about through the efforts of the church, and during this golden age the church, not Israel, will experience the fulfillment of the promises to Abraham and David. The kingdom will be on earth, but it will be a "church kingdom" not a Jewish kingdom, and the King, Christ, will be absent from the earth, not present on it. He will rule in the hearts of the people and return to the earth only after the millennium is complete. Then will follow a general resurrection of all the dead, a general judgment of all people, and eternity will begin.

Postmillennialism conceives of the unfulfilled Abrahamic promises as being fulfilled by the church and, of course, not in any literal sense. Its method of interpretation is generally to spiritualize prophecy. The postmillennial scheme looks like this:

AMILLENNIALISM

This viewpoint teaches that there will be no millennium at all in the future. Whatever kingdom there is, is now — it is heaven's rule over the church. Conditions in this present age will become increasingly worse until the second coming of Christ at the end of this church age, and the return of the Lord will be immediately followed by a general resurrection and judgment and the commencement of the eternal state.

Amillennialists have three different ways of explaining the fulfillment of the Abrahamic covenant. Some say that the land promises were fulfilled completely during the reign of Solomon who did have much of the promised territory under tribute (1 Ki 4:21). However, he did not possess the total

extent of the land, and certainly it was not possessed forever
as the covenant promised. Others insist that the covenant
was conditional and therefore the unfulfilled promises of the
covenant do not have to be fulfilled since Israel was disobedient and thus sinned away her right to the promises. Still
others (probably the majority) feel that the church fulfills
the promises in a nonliteral way. Christ is now seated on the
throne of David in heaven and is fulfilling to the church the
necessary essence of the Old Testament promises. Amillennialists seem to feel the force of the importance of doing
something with the covenant promises.

Amillennial interpretation spiritualizes the promises made
to Israel as a nation when they say that they are fulfilled by
the church. According to this view, Revelation 20 describes
the scene of souls in heaven during the time between the
first and second comings of Christ. The amillennial scheme
looks like this:

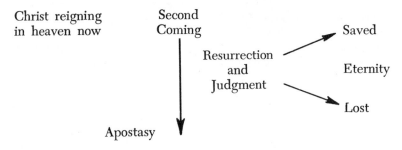

PREMILLENNIALISM

Premillennialists hold that the second coming of Christ
will occur before (pre) the millennium and that Christ, not
the church (as in postmillennialism) will be the one to establish the kingdom. Christ will actually reign over the
earth as King, and during the millennium the Jewish people
will experience the fulfillment of the promises made to Abraham and David. According to premillennialism, the present
church age will see increasing apostasy which will climax
in the time of tribulation before the second coming of Christ.

When He returns He will set up His kingdom for 1,000 years after which will occur the resurrection and judgment of the unsaved and the ushering in of eternity.

The premillennial scheme is a result of interpreting the promises and prophecies of Scripture in a plain, normal or literal way. This is the strength of premillennialism — its method of interpretation is consistently the same whether applied to history, doctrine or prophecy. It is unwise to take the words of the Bible in a nonliteral sense, particularly when the literal meaning is plain. Those promises to Abraham and David concerned the physical descendants of Abraham. Why, then, expect them to be fulfilled by the church unless Israel no longer means Israel but by some sleight of hand means the church? Since the New Testament continues to distinguish the Jews from the church, it appears that we can expect these promises to be fulfilled through the Jews rather than the church (1 Co 10:32; Ro 11:26). The premillennial scheme looks like this:

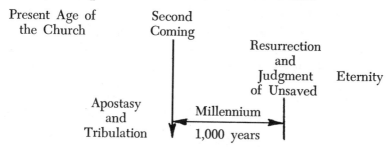

THE RAPTURE OF THE CHURCH

THE DESCRIPTION OF THE RAPTURE (JN 14:1-3; 1 CO 15:51-57; 1 TH 4:13-18)

The title "rapture" comes from the Latin word used in 1 Thessalonians 4:17 which is translated in English "caught up." The rapture of the church is the catching up or translation of the church. It is the catching up to the dwelling place promised in John 14:1-3. In the Corinthians passage

Paul says this is a mystery. That word "mystery" ought to be like a red flag reminding us that this is something not known before but now revealed. Resurrection was no mystery, for the Old Testament taught clearly that men would be raised from the dead (Job 19:25; Is 26:19; Dan 12:2), but it did not reveal that a number of people would go into God's presence without experiencing death. That is why "we shall not all sleep" is a mystery (1 Co 15:51). At the rapture some mortals (living) will only need to put on immortality, while those whose bodies have seen corruption (dead) will need to put on incorruption through resurrection. Both routes to heaven involve change — the living need to be translated and the dead raised. The last generation of Christians will not experience death.

These changes will occur "in a moment, in the twinkling of an eye." The rapture will be instantaneous, not gradual, for the Greek word translated "moment" is the term from which our word "atom" comes. Because when the atom was discovered it was thought to be indivisible, it was named "atom." Even though the atom has been split, the word still means "indivisible," and indicates that the rapture will occur in an indivisible instant of time. Furthermore, Paul says that we shall *all* be changed, not *part* of the company of believers. Thus 1 Corinthians 15:51-58 teaches three things: (1) The rapture will include not only the bodily resurrection of those believers who have died, but also the changing of the bodies of those who are alive at the time it happens. (2) It will be instantaneous. (3) It will include all believers, not simply some of them.

But it is 1 Thessalonians 4:13-18 that gives the most detail about what will happen when the Lord returns. Four things are featured in this passage:

1. Christ Himself will return (v. 16), and the attendant circumstances will include all the grandeur His personal presence deserves. There will be a shout of command, the voice of an (not *the*) archangel, and the trumpet of God.

2. There will be a resurrection (v. 16). The dead will be raised and the living changed, all in the twinkling of an eye. However, only the dead in Christ and living Christians will experience the rapture, not all people. There is not one general resurrection, but several, this one involving only believers.

3. There will be a rapture (v. 17). The word means the act of conveying a person from one place to another, and is therefore quite properly used in this passage of conveying living persons to heaven (see 2 Co 12:4).

4. There will be reunions (v. 17) both with loved ones who have previously died in the Lord and with the Lord Himself. And all these reunions will be forever.

THE TIME OF THE RAPTURE

Almost all agree that the rapture is to be distinguished from the second coming in the sense that the former is when Christ comes for His own people and the latter is His coming with them in triumph and glory. But how far apart these two events are in time is the disputed question. Amillennialists believe that they both occur at the close of the tribulation days but that the rapture is *immediately* followed by the second coming (which is immediately followed by eternity without any millennium). Among premillennialists there are four views of the time of the rapture.

Posttribulation view. The posttribulationalists teach the same thing as amillennialists concerning the chronological relation of the rapture and the second coming (except that in posttribulationalism the second coming is followed by the millennium). According to this viewpoint the church will be present on earth during the tribulation period, and the comings for and with His saints occur in quick succession at the close of that period. Their principal arguments for this are:

1. The rapture and the second coming are described in the Scriptures by the same words, which indicates that they occur at the same time (1 Th 4:15 and Mt 24:27).

2. Since saints are mentioned as present during the tribulation days, the church is present on earth during that time (Mt 24:22).

3. It is predicted that a resurrection will occur at the beginning of the millennium, and since it is assumed that this is the same resurrection as that which occurs at the rapture, the rapture will take place just before the millennium (Rev 20:4).

4. The church can and will be preserved from the wrath of the tribulation period by supernatural protection while living through that time and not by deliverance from the period (as Israel was protected from the plagues while living in Egypt).

5. The Scriptures do not teach imminency; therefore, the rapture can be after the known events of the tribulation.

6. Posttribulationalism was the position of the early church.

Midtribulation. The midtribulationalists believe that Christ's coming for His people will occur at the middle point of the tribulation period — that is 3½ years after it begins and 3½ years before the end at which time the Lord will return with His saints to set up His millennial kingdom. The arguments for this concept are:

1. The last trumpet of 1 Corinthians 15:52 is the same as the seventh trumpet of Revelation 11:15, and it is sounded at the middle of the tribulation.

2. Actually, the great tribulation is only the last half of Daniel's seventieth week, and the church is promised deliverance only from that (Rev 11:2; 12:6).

3. The resurrection of the two witnesses pictures the rapture of the church, and their resurrection occurs at the middle of the tribulation (Rev 11:11).

Partial rapture. The partial rapturists teach that only those believers who are worthy will be taken out of the world before the tribulation begins, while others will be left to endure its wrath. For those left on earth, that time will serve as a time of purging. The idea is taken from verses like Hebrews 9:28 which seem to require preparedness as a prequisite for meeting the Lord. The viewpoint is based on the idea that good works are necessary in order to qualify to be raptured, but the question is not answered, how many good works? Also, it seems to ignore the fact that 1 Corinthians 15:51 (ASV) says plainly that "we shall all be changed" in the rapture.

Pretribulation. The pretribulationalists hold that the rapture of the church will take place before the entire seven-year tribulation period begins. Then, seven years later, after the conclusion of the tribulation, the Lord will return to earth with His people to set up His millennial kingdom. Pretribulationalists base their conclusions on these arguments:

1. The tribulation is called "the great day of his wrath" (Rev 6:17). Believers, who know the Deliverer from the wrath to come (1 Th 1:10), are assured that God has not appointed them to wrath (1 Th 5:9). Since in the context of this latter verse Paul was speaking about the *beginning* of the day of the Lord or of the tribulation period (1 Th 5:2), it seems clear that he is saying that Christians will not be present during any part of that time of wrath but will be removed before any of it begins. That could only be true if the rapture is before the tribulation.

2. The risen Lord promised the church at Philadelphia to "keep thee from the hour of temptation, which shall come upon all the world, to try them that dwell upon the earth" (Rev 3:10). Pretribulationalists relate this promise, like promises made in other letters to local churches, to the whole church (though obviously it will be experienced only by believers living when Christ comes), and they understand that the "hour of temptation" refers to the tribulation since it is said in the verse to be worldwide. Posttribulationalists claim that this promise (which they also relate to the tribulation) means only that Christians will be protected from

the judgments of the tribulation, even though they will have
to live through the time. However, it is important to notice
that the promise is not only to keep *from* (and the preposition does mean *from*, not *in*) the trouble, but to keep from
the *hour* (or time) of trouble. That seems to say complete
exemption from being anywhere around during the time. It
is well known that the phrase "keep from" is used only twice
in the New Testament — here and in John 17:15. In the latter reference the Lord prayed that believers would be kept
from the evil one, which prayer is answered by delivering us
from the power of darkness and transferring us into the
kingdom of His dear Son (Col 1:13). It is impossible to conceive of being in the location where something is happening
and being exempt from the time of the happening. Furthermore, since the tribulation will be worldwide, exemption
would necessitate removal from the earth before it begins.

Now, if the posttribulationalists be correct, then this promise will have to be reinterpreted in some other way by them,
for many saints in the tribulation days will *not* be protected
from the persecutions while living through the period, for we
know that many will die for their faith (Rev 6:9-11; 7:9-14;
14:1-3; 15:1-3).

3. Second Thessalonians 2:1-12 sets up an important
chronological sequence. Paul says that the day of the Lord
cannot come (i.e., the tribulation cannot begin) until cer-
tian things happen (v. 3). One is that the man of sin must be
revealed first (v. 3). But the man of sin cannot be revealed
until something (v. 6, where the neuter is used) and someone (v. 7, where the masculine is used) are taken out of the
way. Then and only then can the man of sin appear to do
his evil work. Whatever or whoever the restrainer is, he is
holding back the full manifestation of the man of sin. The
Thessalonians knew what or who the restrainer is. In addition, it appears that he must be stronger than Satan since
the man of sin is empowered by Satan. Most commentators
identify the restrainer with the Roman Empire of Paul's

day with its advanced legal system. But was it or is any government more powerful than Satan? Only God is that, so behind whatever things that restrain must be the all-powerful person of God who Himself restrains. Undoubtedly God uses good government, elect angels, the influence of the Bible and other means to restrain evil, but the ultimate power behind anything that restrains must be the power and person of God. Many pretribulationalists identify the Holy Spirit as the particular Person of the Godhead whose work it is to restrain (see Gen 6:3). Whether Paul is specifically referring to the Holy Spirit in this passage may be uncertain. However, whether we can make that specific identification or not does not affect the pretribulation argument from this passage. It goes like this:

The Restrainer is God, and the principal instrument of restraint is the God-indwelt church (see Eph 4:6; Gal 2:20; 1 Co 6:19). Our Lord declared of the divinely indwelt and empowered church that "the gates of hell shall not prevail against it" (Mt 16:18). The restrainer must be removed before the man of sin can be revealed and before the day of the Lord can begin. Since the Restrainer is ultimately God, and since God indwells all believers, either He must be withdrawn from the hearts of His people while they are left on earth to go through the tribulation, or else when He is withdrawn, all believers must be taken with Him in the rapture. The Bible nowhere even hints that Christians can be disindwelt, so the only alternative is that they will be taken out of the world before the tribulation begins. This does not mean that the Holy Spirit will not be working during that time. His presence will be here, but His residence will be removed when the church is taken. To say that the Restrainer is removed is not to say that the presence or activity of God is taken away from the earth. Many will be redeemed during the tribulation and this will be the work of God (Rev 7:14). Thus a proper interpretation of this passage involves a pretribulation rapture of the church.

THE TRIBULATION PERIOD

The Bible says a great deal in both Old and New Testaments about the tribulation period — more than about many other doctrines.

ITS LENGTH

The period is the seventieth week of Daniel's great prophecy recorded in Daniel 9:24-27. Half of the time is said to be 42 months or 1,260 days (Rev 11:2-3). This, of course, is based on 30-day months which has sometimes been considered as an invention of students of prophecy. Notice, however, that 30-day months are found in nonprophetic passages such as Genesis 7:11, 24 and 8:4, and Numbers 20:29, Deuteronomy 34:8 and 21:13 where a 30-day period of mourning was called a full month. This 7-year period is divided into two equal parts by the breaking of the treaty which will be made at the beginning (Dan 9:27). Both parts will be characterized by intense persecution and judgment.

ITS UNIQUENESS

Our Lord spoke of the tribulation days as unique in the entire history of the world (Mt 24:21). Of course there have been many difficult times since these words were spoken, the Lord Himself even warning that His followers would have tribulation in this world (Jn 16:33). What is it then that makes this coming period unique?

Two characteristics will distinguish the tribulation from all other times of persecution and judgment that the world has seen. First, it will be worldwide, not localized (Rev 3:10). Therefore, terrible as they are, the persecutions which people are experiencing in parts of the world today cannot indicate that the tribulation has come, for that time will affect the entire world. Second, the tribulation will be unique because then people will not only realize that the end of the world is near but they will act like it. In one of the early judgments, men will hide themselves in the dens and caves of the mountains and say, "Fall on us, and hide us from the face of him that sitteth on the throne, and from the wrath of the Lamb" (Rev 6:16). Often men have talked as if the end were near. Many even today use the word Armageddon as a symbol of the end. But people are not acting as if they really believed that the end is at hand. Real estate is changing hands and savings are being accumulated as if life will continue indefinitely. When the tribulation comes, men will prefer death to life, for the future will hold no attraction.

ITS DESCRIPTION

The tribulation actually begins when the man of sin, the leader of the western federation of nations, signs a treaty with the Jewish people (Dan 9:27). The rapture of the church will have occurred just before this, though there may be a short interval of time between the rapture and the signing. It is the signing that actually begins the countdown of the seven years. There are three series of judgments recorded in Revelation 6, 8-9, 16. Probably they are successive, following one another in chronological sequence (rather than some of them recapitulating what has already been revealed). If so, then the seal judgments of chapter 6 will come during the first years of the tribulation. They involve war, famine, death, martyrdom and disturbances in the physical universe.

At the same early part of the period the great ecumenical apostate church will rise to power (Rev 17:3), exerting tremendous political influence among the nations of the world. In addition there will be many converted by the witness of the group that will be sealed (Rev 7) for this purpose. Some will apparently be martyred almost immediately for their faith (Rev 6:9-11). All of this was indicated by the Lord in the Olivet discourse (Mt 24:4-14 — the judgment, vv. 6-7; the martyrs, v. 9; the witnessing, v. 14).

As the middle of the tribulation approaches, certain important events will occur. Egypt will be defeated by the armies of the man of sin (Dan 11:40-43). The nations of the Far East will be forming into a coalition and will at the end of the tribulation move into Palestine. The power bloc to the north of Palestine known as Gog and Magog will invade Palestine but will be wiped out by God's supernatural intervention (Eze 38-39). Exactly at the middle point the man of sin will break his treaty, cease to be Israel's protector, demand to be worshiped himself (2 Th 2:4), and seek to conquer the world. In the meantime, as the latter part of the tribulation progresses, God will be pouring out additional judgments on the world. These are described in the trumpets of Revelation 8-9 and the bowls of chapter 16. They include more disturbances in the physical universe, including the water supply of people, mass deaths, demonic persecution, pain and sores, and widespread havoc and destruction. As the man of sin continues his march to world power, he will face his enemies from the east at Armageddon in northern Palestine. In the midst of the war the Lord will return and defeat all His enemies. The man of sin and his false prophet will be cast into the lake of fire to be tormented forever.

Why must there be such a time as this? There are at least two reasons: First, the wickedness of man must be punished. Even though God may seem to be doing nothing about evil now, someday He will act openly against it. Second, man must, by one means or another, be prostrated before the King of kings and Lord of lords. He may do so voluntarily now by coming to Christ in faith and receiving salvation, or he will have to bow later but then only to receive condemnation, not salvation.

THE MILLENNIAL KINGDOM

ITS CHARACTER

The millennial kingdom is that period of 1,000 years during which our Lord Jesus Christ will rule the earth in righteousness and will fulfill to the Jews and the world those promises of the Old Testament covenants. While the duration of that kingdom as 1,000 years is stated in only one passage (Rev 20, but 6 times in the chapter), the kingdom is the subject of many verses in both Old and New Testaments. The subject is not confined — as is often charged — to one chapter in a book of the Bible that is difficult to interpret.

The kingdom is designated in the Bible in various ways. It is called the kingdom that is coming in the Lord's prayer (Mt 6:10), the kingdom of God (Lk 19:11), the kingdom of Christ (Rev 11:15), the regeneration (Mt 19:28), the times of refreshing (Ac 3:19), and the world to come (Heb 2:5). Our Lord indicated in the parable of Luke 19:11-27 that the kingdom would not be set up immediately, implying clearly that something else (the church) would come first in the plan of God before the kingdom would be established.

ITS GOVERNMENT

The millennial government will, of course, be set up on this earth (Zec 14:9). The topography of the earth will have been changed by the time the kingdom becomes functional because of the catastrophic judgments of the tribulation period (earthquakes, drastic climatic changes, etc.). The city of Jerusalem will be the center of the government (Is 2:3). That city will be exalted (Zec 14:10); it will be a place of great glory (Is 24:23); the site of the temple will be there (Is 33:20); and Jerusalem will be the joy of the whole earth (Ps 48:2). Furthermore, though now the center of so much dispute and conflict, in the millennium Jerusalem will never again need to fear for her safety (Is 26:1-4). From that capital shall go forth the law, and the earth shall be full of the knowledge of the Lord as the waters cover the sea (Is 2:3; 11:9).

The Lord will be the King of the millennial theocracy. As

King, He will rule all the earth (Dan 7:14), and the result
will be perfect and complete justice for all His subjects. He
will punish sin (Is 11:4; 65:20), and He will judge in perfect righteousness (Is 11:3-5). This is the secret of peace on
earth — a Ruler who can enforce peace righteously. Apparently the Lord will use resurrected David as a regent (Jer
30:9; Eze 37:24-25) — a prince under the authority of the
King. Authority over the twelve tribes of Israel will be
vested in the hands of the twelve apostles (Mt 19:28), and
other princes and nobles will likewise share in the governmental duties (Jer 30:21; Is 32:1). Many lesser people will
have responsibilities in various departments of the millennial
government (Lk 19:11-27).

The subjects of this earthly kingdom will be the people,
Jews and Gentiles, who survive the tribulation period and
enter the millennium in earthly bodies. It would appear that
at the beginning, then, there will be not a single unsaved
person in the kingdom. However, it will not be long — perhaps only minutes — before a baby is born, then another
and another, until in just a few years there will be a large
number of teenagers in the kingdom. Some will accept
Christ as their Saviour, and others will not, though all,
whether regenerated or not, will have to give outward allegiance to the authority of the King. The church will rule
with Christ and will have resurrection bodies. They will not
be subject to physical limitations nor will they contribute to
space, food, or governmental problems during the millennium. The actual residence of the church during the millennium will be the New Jerusalem (Rev 21:2, 9-10).

ITS SPIRITUAL CHARACTER

It is sometimes said that the millennial kingdom cannot be
spiritual because it is earthly, but, of course, there need be
no contradiction between the two ideas. A Christian today
living on earth is expected to be spiritual. Actually, during
the millennium God will join the spiritual and earthly in a

final display of His glory on this earth, and the kingdom will show the highest standards of spirituality.

Some of the spiritual characteristics of the kingdom include the following: Righteousness will flourish (Is 11:3-5), peace will be universal (Is 2:4), the Holy Spirit will be manifest in unusual ways (Is 61:3; Joel 2:28-29), and Satan will be bound (Rev 20:2-3). Some believe that the temple will be rebuilt during the millennium and used for worship with animal sacrifices. Ezekiel 40—46 does seem to indicate this, though the question is often asked, What purpose will such sacrifices serve, since Christ will be actually present on the earth? Perhaps the answer to that question escapes us simply because we do not fully understand all that will be involved in the spiritual worship of the kingdom.

ITS SOCIAL JUSTICE

A theocratic rule of righteousness and justice will include ramifications in the area of social justice during the millennium. No longer will courts have to depend on the usual avenues of evidence — the eyes and ears — which are subject to error, because Christ will judge accurately on the basis of His complete knowledge of everything (Is 11:3-5). No crime will go unpunished; oppression will not be allowed to continue; costs for law enforcement will be drastically cut (thus reducing taxes); and world peace will eliminate expenditures for military purposes.

In addition, the productivity of the earth will be greatly increased (Is 35:1-2) because the curse to which the earth was subjected after the sin of Adam (Gen 3:17) will be reversed, though it will not be entirely lifted until the end of the millennium when death will finally and forever be vanquished. Increased rainfall, food and productivity will, of course, bring in an era of great prosperity for all, and Christ's just rule will guarantee that all are properly paid for, whatever they produce by way of products or services. Peace on earth will mean prosperity on earth and social justice for all.

ITS END

The end of the millennium will see the last and final revolt of man and Satan against God and His rule. For a thousand years God will have given all mankind the most ideal conditions under which to live and will have spread the knowledge of the Lord throughout the world. The fact that men will openly oppose God after such benefits will serve to prove that change in outward conditions does not meet man's basic need. Inside he still will be a rebel unless he has had a change of heart through regeneration. Many who will be born during the millennium will not choose to receive the saving grace of the King. All will apparently be obliged to give outward allegiance to Christ, but, as in every age, God will not compel men to receive the Saviour. Consequently, many living at the conclusion of the millennium will not have trusted Christ for salvation even though they will have obeyed Him as Head of the government.

The opportunity to revolt against Christ will come when Satan will be loosed (Rev 20:7-9). As soon as this happens he will deceive the nations as he did before being confined, and his influence will be worldwide. His revolution will gather momentum as the rebellious forces head for the capital city, Jerusalem, to strike at the very center of Christ's government. Just as they are about to attack, God will send fire from heaven to destroy them completely. That will end forever opposition of all kinds to the Lord. The people who join this revolt will be destroyed by fire. Satan will be cast into the lake of fire (Rev 20:10). Reformation is not the same as regeneration, and betterment is not conversion; this last revolt will prove once again that it is the heart of man that needs a work of supernatural grace.

THE JUDGMENTS OF THE FUTURE

THE JUDGMENT OF BELIEVERS' WORKS

After the church is taken to heaven through translation and resurrection, individual believers will be judged for their works done as Christians (1 Co 3:11-15). Salvation with its assurance of heaven is not in question, only whether heaven will be entered with or without rewards. Paul makes it quite clear in this passage that those believers whose works are of the character that they do not pass the test will nevertheless be saved (v. 15). The question is often raised how one's sins can be forgiven and yet one's deeds reviewed at the judgment seat of Christ. Forgiveness concerns justification; the review concerns rewards, and after the review is made there will be no sorrow or tears because there are none in heaven. Too, we often wonder what the nature of the rewards will be. If heaven is heaven, what difference will rewards make? The answer to that is not given in the Bible; nevertheless, rewards are mentioned as a proper motivation for Christian service. We are told for what things rewards will be given. A crown of rejoicing will be given for bringing people to Christ (1 Th 2:19); a crown of righteousness, for loving His appearing (2 Ti 4:8); a crown of life, for enduring testing with love for the Lord (Ja 1:12), and a crown of glory to elders who are faithful to their responsibilities in the church (1 Pe 5:4).

THE JUDGMENT OF GENTILES WHO SURVIVE

THE TRIBULATION

Some people will live through the judgments of the tribulation period, and they will be judged before the millennium is set up and functioning. The time of the judgment is clearly indicated as "when the Son of man shall come in his glory" (Mt 25:31-46). It will take place on the earth in the valley of Jehoshaphat (Joel 3:2). Probably this valley will be created in the area of Jerusalem by some of the physical disruptions connected with the second coming of Christ (Zec 14:4). Those judged are called the "nations," a Hebrew word translated "people," "heathen," "nations," and, most often, "Gentiles." The Greek word translated "nations" in Matthew 25:32 is also often translated "Gentiles" in the New Testament (see Ro 11:11-12, 25). This must be a judg-

ment of individuals (there has never been a righteous nation), not nations as groups, so it is best to translate "Gentiles."

The basis of judging will be the treatment by these Gentiles of a group which the Lord Jesus called "my brethren"
(Mt 25:40). Who these are can be determined by a process
of elimination. Since Christ is present as Judge, since the
church has been raptured before the tribulation begins,
since living Gentiles are being judged, the only group left
would seem to be the Jews of the tribulation times (His
"brethren" according to the flesh). They will be the objects
of intense persecution during those days, so that anyone who
befriends them or does any act of kindness to them will himself come under great suspicion. People will not feed,
clothe or visit Jews simply for humanitarian reasons during
that time. To do these things will involve a real risk of one's
own life, so doing these things will therefore be evidence of
new life in the doer's heart. In other words, the works of
kindness which these Gentiles will have done for the Jewish
brethren of the Lord will prove the regenerated condition
of the Gentiles. Being regenerted saves them; doing these
good works proves that they are regenerated.

Those whose lives have given evidence of the new birth
will become citizens of the kingdom (Mt 25:34). Those
whose works proved their lack of eternal life will be condemned to the lake of fire (v. 41). Those who do enter the
kingdom will enter with their earthly bodies; they will
marry, bear children and become the means of populating
the millennial earth.

THE JUDGMENT OF JEWS WHO SURVIVE THE TRIBULATION

Those Jews who live through the tribulation period will
also be judged (Eze 20:34-38). The Lord also spoke of this
judgment in a parable (Mt 25:14-30) and placed it immediately after His return. The result of this judgment will be
that the unsaved Jews will be cut off from both millennial

and eternal life, for no rebel will enter the millennium (Eze 20:37; Mt 25:30).

THE JUDGMENT OF FALLEN ANGELS

Satan will, of course, be judged at the second coming of Christ by being bound in the abyss during the millennium and then after his brief revolt at the conclusion be cast eternally into the lake of fire (Rev 20:2-3, 7, 10). Those angels who followed Satan's initial revolt against God will also be judged. The time is called "the great day" (Jude 6) — probably at the conclusion of the millennium (the end of the day of the Lord) when Satan is finally judged. Believers will apparently have a part in executing this judgment (1 Co 6:3).

THE JUDGMENT OF THE UNSAVED DEAD
(AT THE GREAT WHITE THRONE) (REV 20:11-15)

At the conclusion of the millennial reign a great white throne will be established somewhere in space, for the present earth and starry heavens will have been replaced. The Judge who will sit on this throne will be Christ (Jn 5:22 — the better texts of Rev 20:12 read "before the throne," not "before God"). Those who are judged will be the unsaved dead of all time. All the redeemed will have been raised and judged previously, so only the unsaved are left (Rev 20:6).

These people will also be judged on the basis of their works (vv. 12-13). They get into this judgment because they are unsaved, but once there, they are judged for their works. When the book of life is opened, it will be seen that no name of anyone standing before the throne appears in it. Rejection of the Saviour has kept their names out of the book of life. Their works done during their lifetimes prove that these people deserve eternal punishment.

It is almost an act of condescension on God's part to show men at this judgment that they deserve the lake of fire on the basis of their own personal records. It seems likely, too, that this basis of judgment will also serve as a basis for different degrees of punishment in hell (see Lk 12:47-48). For all who stand in this judgment, the result will be the same — they will be cast into the lake of fire. This is called the second death and means eternal separation from God. Even death (which claims the body) and hades (which claims the soul) will be cast into the lake of fire, for their work will be finished.

Charted, these future judgments look like this:

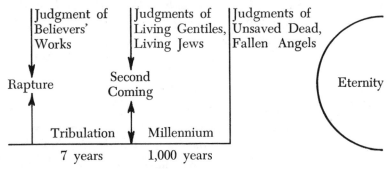

THE RESURRECTIONS

Contrary to popular ideas, there will not be one general resurrection day. Basically there are two resurrections when considered in relation to classes of people involved, not chronology — the resurrection of the just and the resurrection of the unjust (Jn 5:28-29; Lk 14:14).

Between the death of the body and the resurrection, both the righteous and wicked exist in a conscious state. The believer is in the presence of the Lord during this time (2 Co 5:1-8; Phil 1:23) while the unbeliever is in conscious torment (Lk 16:19-31).

THE RESURRECTION OF THE JUST

The resurrection of the just is also called the first resurrection and will occur in several stages, not all at once. The dead in Christ will be raised first at the rapture of the church

(1 Th 4:16). The redeemed of the tribulation period who die during that time will be raised before the millennium (Rev 20:4). The redeemed of Old Testament times will also be a part of the resurrection of the just. Expositors are divided over when they will be raised, some believing that it will happen at the rapture when the church saints are raised, and others holding that it will occur at the second coming (Dan 12:2 – the writer prefers the latter view).

THE RESURRECTION OF THE UNJUST

As indicated above in discussing the judgment of the great white throne, all unsaved people of all time will be raised after the millennium to be judged and then cast into the lake of fire forever (Rev 20:11-15). At their resurrection they will apparently be given some sort of bodies that will be able to live forever and feel the effects of the torments of the lake of fire.

HEAVEN AND HELL

HEAVEN

The Scriptures speak of the heavens (Gen 1:1; Heb 4:14) and there are apparently only three (2 Co 12:2 – the third heaven being the actual presence of God). Our Lord referred to heaven as a definite place (Jn 14:1-3), entrance into which is only through Christ.

Some of the characteristics of heaven are as follows: It is inhabited (Heb 12:22-24), it is a place of great beauty (Rev 21:1 – 22:7), there will be no reproduction there (Mk 12:25), it is a holy place (Rev 21:27), we will serve and worship and fellowship with God there (Rev 4–5), and being in heaven will give us a new perspective on everything (see Is 66:24).

HELL

The English word *hell* is quite unspecific in comparison

with the biblical words which it often translates. In the Old Testament the word *hell* translates the Hebrew word *sheol,* which sometimes means the grave and sometimes the place of departed people in contrast to the state of the living. It was regarded as a place of horror (Ps 30:9; Num 16:33), weeping (Is 38:3), and punishment (Job 24:19).

In the New Testament there are three words which relate to the doctrine of hell. *Hades* is the equivalent to *Sheol* and is the place where unsaved people go when they die to await their resurrection and judgment at the great white throne. *Hades* is temporary in that it will be cast into the lake of fire. *Tartaros* (2 Pe 2:4) occurs only one time and describes the place where certain fallen angels are confined. *Gehenna* (2 Ki 23:10 and Mt 10:28) was a common refuse dump and a place of perpetual fire and loathsomeness, and the valley in Jerusalem illustrates the fire and awfulness of the lake of fire. Hell is conceived of as a place of outer darkness (Mt 8:12), eternal torment and punishment (Rev 14:10-11).

The punishment of the unsaved is not annihilation, nor will they be restored after some time of punishment. In other words, the Bible does not allow for conditional immortality (final annihilation) or classic universalism (restoration after a time of punishment). The same word that is used for eternal judgment (Heb 6:2), is used for eternal life (Jn 3:15), and for the eternal God (1 Ti 1:17). If one of these is temporary, then the others must be too. Furthermore, the same phrase that means *forever* is used of God being alive forever (Rev 15:7), of eternal life (Jn 10:28) and of eternal torment (Rev 14:11). Again there is no way to escape the conclusion that if God is everlasting, so is punishment in the lake of fire. There is no annihilation and no restoration. Universalism today often takes the form of teaching that all will be saved without any kind of punishment. It is based on misinterpretations of Acts 3:21, 1 Corinthians 15:24-28 and Colossians 1:20, but it completely ignores the biblical teaching of the diverse destinies of the righteous and wicked (Mt 25:46; Jn 5:29; Ro 2:8-10; Rev 20:10, 15).

Notes

Chapter 2

1. Ray Summers, "How God Said It," *Baptist Standard,* Feb. 4, 1970, p. 12.
2. F. F. Bruce, *Are the New Testament Documents Reliable?* (Chicago: Inter-Varsity, 1943), pp. 16-17.

Chapter 3

1. J. Oliver Buswell, *A Systematic Theology of the Christian Religion* (Grand Rapids: Zondervan, 1962), 1:105.
2. John F. Walvoord, *Jesus Christ Our Lord* (Chicago: Moody, 1969), p. 137.

Chapter 4

1. B. F. Westcott, *The Gospel According to St. John* (Greenwood, S.C.: Attic Press, 1958), 2:219.
2. See the more complete discussion of this in Charles C. Ryrie, *Balancing the Christian Life* (Chicago: Moody, 1969), pp. 163-68.
3. G. G. Findlay, *Expositor's Greek Testament* (Grand Rapids: Eerdmans, n.d.), 2:896.

Chapter 5

1. C. L. Feinberg, *The Prophecy of Ezekiel* (Chicago: Moody, 1969), p. 161.
2. See the discussion of voodoo in "Haiti," in *The West Indies,* Life World Library (New York: Time, 1963), pp. 55 ff.
3. A good discussion appears in J. Stafford Wright, *Man in the Process of Time* (Grand Rapids: Eerdmans, 1956), pp. 128-36.

Chapter 6

1. H. Graham Cannon, *The Evolution of Living Things* (Springfield, Ill.: Thomas, 1958), p. 92.
2. Earnest A. Hooton, *Up from the Ape* Rev. ed. (New York: Macmillan, 1946), p. 56.
3. Alfred S. Romer, in *Genetics, Palaeontology and Evolution,* ed. Glenn L. Jepsen, et al. (New York: Athenium, 1963), p. 114.
4. For a full discussion of this question read John C. Whitcomb and Henry M. Morris, *The Genesis Flood* (Philadelphia: Presbyterian and Reformed, 1960), pp. 1-35.
5. Archibald M. Hunter, *Interpreting Paul's Gospel* (Philadelphia: Westminster, 1967), p. 77.

6. Personally I doubt that the words, "neither shall ye touch it" in v. 3 are an addition to God's words to Adam and Eve simply because it is difficult to conceive of Eve lying and therefore sinning before eating the forbidden fruit.

Chapter 7

1. James H. Moulton and George Milligan, *The Vocabulary of the Greek Testament* (Grand Rapids: Eerdmans, 1949), p. 65; and Gustaf Deismann, *Light from the Ancient East* (New York: Harper, n.d.), pp. 152-53.

2. Frank Stagg, *New Testament Theology* (Nashville: Broadman, 1962), pp. 135-36.

3. Ibid., p. 145.

4. Amos N. Wilder, *New Testament Faith for Today* (New York: Harper, 1955), p. 134.

5. For further elaboration, see Charles C. Ryrie, *Biblical Theology of the New Testament* (Chicago: Moody, 1959), pp. 256-58.

6. J. I. Packer, *Evangelism and the Sovereignty of God* (Chicago: Inter-Varsity, 1961), p. 89.

7. Archibald T. Robertson, *Word Pictures in the New Testament* (Nashville: Broadman, 1943), 3:35-36.

Chapter 8

1. For a complete discussion of the matter, see Charles C. Ryrie, *The Role of Women in the Church* (Chicago: Moody, 1968), pp. 85-91.

2. Alfred Edersheim, *The Life and Times of Jesus the Messiah* (Grand Rapids: Eerdmans, 1953), 2:745-47.

Helpful Books on Bible Doctrine

Among the many books on Bible doctrine and the many systematic theologies, the author has found these that are listed to be helpful for use in further study or in teaching this subject.

Barackman, Floyd Hays. *Practical Christian Theology.* Old Tappan, N.J.: Revell, 1981.

Buswell, James Oliver. *A Systematic Theology of the Christian Religion.* Grand Rapids: Zondervan, 1962.

Chafer, Lewis Sperry. Revised by John F. Walvoord. *Major Bible Themes.* Grand Rapids: Zondervan, 1974.

Criswell, W. A. *Great Doctrines of the Bible.* 3 vols. Grand Rapids: Zondervan, 1982-83.

Evans, William. *The Great Doctrines of the Bible.* Rev. ed. Chicago: Moody, 1974.

Gerstner, John H. *Theology for Everyman.* Chicago: Moody, 1965.

Hammond, T. C. *In Understanding Be Men.* London: Inter-Varsity, 1944.

Henry, Carl F. H., ed. *Basic Christian Doctrines.* New York: Holt, Rinehart & Winston, 1962.

Lewis, Gordon R. *Decide for Yourself.* Downers Grove, Ill.: Inter-Varsity, 1970.

Little, Paul E. *Know What You Believe.* Wheaton, Ill.: Scripture Press, 1970.

Pentecost, J. Dwight. *Things Which Become Sound Doctrine.* Westwood, N.J.: Revell, 1965.

Thiessen, Henry C. Revised by Vernon D. Doerksen. *Lectures in Systematic Theology.* Grand Rapids: Eerdmans, 1979.

Subject Index

Scripture Index

Moody Press, a ministry of the Moody Bible Institute, is designed for education, evangelization and edification. If we may assist you in knowing more about Christ and the Christian life, please write us without obligation to: Moody Press, c/o MLM, Chicago, Illinois 60610.